BLACK GOLD
BLACK SCORPION

Biafra remembered

George S Boughton

First published 2015
Published by GB Publishing.org

A catalogue record of the printed book is available from
the British Library

Cover Design © Mary Pargeter Design

GBP

GB Publishing.org
www.gbpublishing.org

For
Pam and Natasha

Acknowledgements
This is for all those whose tribes or other allegiances that struggle with the democratisation process – which western leaders have advocated for good humanitarian reasons (as well as to break Britain's monopoly on trade) but, it has often been rushed. It has been tempting for political elites and professional politicians everywhere to take this as a license for outright power.

My thanks for their encouragement go to Keith and Sheila Futcher, Brenda Marsh and Juliette Foster

iii

Contents

Map of Biafra   **1**

Port Harcourt   **3**

1   We were startled in our sleep by an explosion   5
2   It was 'dry' in that it didn't rain, much   10
3   Oh, de bomb not be for you   16
4   We were hostages   21
5   We got into wooden canoes and paddled hard   29
6   You leave next week   32

Midwest Nigeria   **35**

7   A gélè, expressed everything   37
8   SHELL ENGINEER YOU GO PASS DIS PLACE YOU GO DIE O   47
9   Dere be people hurt here!   51
10 We sensed no hostility   59
11 One of the Babies flew through   67

Port Harcourt   **79**

12 I have to kill the Ibos   81
13 You bring the girl who is not there   98

Lagos   **105**

14 I read Ojukwu's book...He was right   107
15 A complex man, in a complex situation   126
16 Tyres smoking on the roadside   132

The Author   **136**

Other 2013-14 GBP Publications   **137**

Map of Biafra

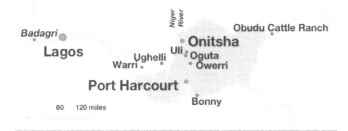

Map of the Republic of Biafra upon secession from Nigeria

Biafran War
30 May 1967 to 15 January 1970

'We aim at everything that moves...

we will aim at everything even if it is not moving'

:Black Scorpion

In the first year of war –
(as ordered by the Nigerian government)
(* A few photos came out with mercenaries flying for the Biafrans)

Correspondents' access to Biafra*:   **NONE**
(news blackout)

Access for humanitarian assistance: **NONE**
(Biafra blockaded)

Verifiable accounts of injuries and lives lost: NONE

Throughout the war –
(from figures compiled by aid organisations)
(* Includes survivors of Biafra's boys army, a first among child armies)

Combat deaths overall: **HALF A MILLION**

Deaths by starvation/disease: OVER ONE MILLION

Afflicted children (among survivors)*:   **UNKNOWN**

Port Harcourt

1 *We were startled in our sleep by an explosion*

The first air I breathed in life was African and my first ray of sunshine as a working man was African. No, I wasn't a colonial birth and it wasn't the smell of Shell-BP's promising oilfields that drew me back. Nor was it the luxurious Maracaibo style camp the company had built in the Niger Delta, close to Port Harcourt. The truth is that, prior to landing, Africa was nowhere in my consciousness, had no special meaning to me, especially as a white graduate who'd lived just about everywhere else in the world and had just been recruited as an oilfield engineer by the massive Shell International.

Certainly 'Africa is not easy' was nowhere in my or my newlywed wife's thoughts, and nowhere in our experiences, as we prepared for my debut career. We'd no idea that an attempted genocide was slaughtering well upwards of 10,000 Igbo in the mainly Hausa-Fulani region of Northern Nigeria. Decapitated bodies were flown southeast and thrown out of a trail of planes that then touched down at the Port Harcourt airstrip.

Pam and I landed on the same strip, from honeymooning in the Canary Islands, oblivious of the strife. It was strange enough to walk on a moonless night towards a small building with lights in the windows. There were no other lights.

Suddenly, we were confronted by gleaming white teeth, in faces and eyes so black, and uniforms so darkly camouflaged, that the only other things we made out were their automatic weapons. That was unsettling enough coming from Britain, where nobody in uniform was armed apart from the army; the police weren't and thankfully still aren't normally.

We naturally welcomed being greeted by Shell-BP staff and taken to our new home, a bungalow outside Umukoroshe; until we were startled in our first sleep by an explosion immediately overhead. We catapulted out of bed holding our breaths, and each other, to hear a large creature hopping about on the corrugated roof. It was a vulture. This place, this Africa, certainly had new surroundings for us to acclimatise to, in the wild.

On the very next day we heard of mobs rampaging through the streets, all of it incomprehensible to us, and we were aghast to witness one poor soul being clubbed to death. Our thoughts, as with all expats and most locals who were not directly involved, was for our own safety and with keeping well away. We caught up with what was known about the massacre but had no idea of the scale and ferocity of the reprisals, certainly not from our contact with people and not even from events covered by the local, English language papers. Only in time would it be known that many thousands of Hausas, Tiv and other

Northern Tribes were killed. Millions of people were displaced, as had happened in the north.

It has since been surmised that the north was mainly Islamic and the east mainly Christian, yet apparently the tragic breakup of tribal unity and order did not stem from religious but rather political ideology. Hundreds of disparate tribal chiefs were bound together, within the borders of a sovereign democracy drawn up prior to independence by the British West Africa administration.

That was the culmination of politics through much of the world, with the infrastructures and institutions of foreign interests spreading like tentacles to further trade. In effect it is hard to defend this as anything other than a business approach to world order and, in hindsight, an excessively unilateral one that tribal, religious, communist and other rival interests would and did attack at some stage. Caring societies, which the EU was recognised as when awarded the Nobel Peace Prize, have moved on from this position. A sentiment growing, now, is for ethical values in business – such as promoting *fair trade*.

Britain had ruled by proxy through tribal chiefs, to protect its trade, just as Rome had done across Britannia and Gaul combined. Nigeria is that big. But let's roll the clock back, to see why things became so violently out of hand; to when there was so little contact that the tribes spoke different languages.

As far back as the fall of the Roman and Byzantine Empires those in the north traded at trans-Saharan trading posts, such as that set up by Tuareg camel trains at Kano. While it wasn't until the Elizabethan era, a millennium later, that European merchants circumnavigating the globe set up an Indian transit port and trans-Atlantic trading post in Lagos. By the time Onitsha and then Port Harcourt became trading posts, European missionaries were drawn to educating the still barely clad animists in the east.

All the while trade spiralled upwards, at first with the merchant clippers and then more energetically when steamships and railroads came into being in the industrial revolution. Tribal numbers exploded, like fireworks in an endless Roman Candle, in response to the employment created. In addition skilled tribesmen migrated along trade routes faster than could possibly have been conceived until, suddenly, tribes were encroaching on each other's territories and northern tribes had better educated eastern Igbos competing in their midst. Just as happened when the Romans left Britannia and Gaul, tribal differences flared up without the iron grip of law. Clash!

Would other borders have prevented tribes from warring as their numbers swelled and they mixed along trade routes? Or would those have stopped them fighting over resources such as oil? No, not for long. The key is in understanding that tribes are made of blood, religions of minds and souls, and democracy (unlike military and other forms of government) is not 'turned on' but has to have time to develop generation upon generation by argument and debate but mostly *education*.

2 *It was 'dry' in that it didn't rain, much*

Pam and I remained in the dark about what was going on, or why it was all happening. Sure, there'd been the Mau Mau uprising in Kenya, followed by the Congo crisis; but those conflict zones had been a long way from Nigeria. Besides, we'd not have dreamt of Shell sending us to such a dangerous place. Little did we know... of the ardours of trade – and of Africa's rebirth in the interest of trade – or of the spurt in populations that led to a precipitous clash of hundreds of tribes, tongues and cultures.

Regardless, to us, the expats in Port Harcourt were in no way involved – with any of that. There was also nothing we could do about it except, as a couple, to focus our attention on getting acquainted with our new employer, both in the offices and socially. Shell, the managing partner in the Shell-BP consortium, put much store in those interactions and business had to carry on as usual.

It was the dry season, when there was much activity in building roads for drilling rigs and pipelines for oilfields. Everything would change when the rains came.

The recent turmoil was never out of the papers but, for all that, many in the local communities, covering a vast area, were involved in Shell-BP's activities. They entered into the workplace be it in offices or on roads, a great many under their chiefs, accustomed (yes, from colonial times) to foreigners having zero tolerance for disruptions. That applied whether disruptions were domestic or civil, the hatreds so recently demonstrated being no exception.

Most Nigerians wanted that order with, above all else, gainful employment; and the full focus had to be on this being the dry season when work could get done. When the rainy season would start this was an extremely wet region. Now it was 'dry' only in that it didn't rain, much, but still our clothes clung irritably with perspiration and our faces streamed with sweat – a bane for expat women with makeup who were unaccustomed to the hot humidity.

The real toll on the human body was made apparent to me when playing squash in a really hot court with a fan and no air-conditioning. It was, in effect, like exerting oneself in a sauna. My opponent, a slightly overweight Brit in his twenties, suddenly grabbed his chest and collapsed. Thankfully the camp clinic was close enough that he survived; I heard he'd burst a vessel in his lung and was drowning in his own blood.

I was assigned to surveying oil pipelines, frequently by helicopter, on the look out for leaks – the Ministry of Mines and Power and Shell-BP were fastidious about compensating property owners and, of course, losses in production weren't tolerated either. Standards of vigilance and maintenance were spotlessly high.

Strangely enough, it never occurred to me that in landing anywhere I might be in danger. There was no sense of the terrible violence we've since heard of and, thankfully, we found none of that animosity was ever directed at us.

Naturally enough, quenching a thirst was a must and I quickly appreciated visiting French rigs, such as those of Forex. Where wine was served with meals. I avoided American rigs, which were dry. I also discovered a remarkable thing. You could fly for a long while absolutely anywhere over dense forest and be amazed. On finding a clearing to land in, some small boy or other would run out with a smile and a *cold* beer to sell.

My first challenging experience was to repair a pipe that had ruptured in one of the main oil lines. My first lesson: I had to work it all out by myself, starting with a decision on which clamp to install and taking it out of the materials yard.

By the time I reached the site the Lebanese contractor had already exposed the pipe by digging a bell hole around it, and had stripped the asphalt coating away for the crew to quickly bolt the clamp in place and stop the leak. They'd also pumped oil from the pit. That much they had already been instructed to do by my boss but, as they now advised me, they had not actually fitted a clamp before. Heck, I definitely didn't know. I'd never even seen an oil pipeline, close to. Not letting on, I took the instruction manual from the crate they duly opened. Simple enough. But the Lebanese welders refused to carry on with the next step. Their fear was that, in trying to build a good weld to the oil filled pipe, they might burn too deep and set off an explosion. I had no idea on any of this and was not inclined to force their hand contractually, which left me with no other choice.

I dropped down next to the pipe with them and found their gaze fixed on me. Shrugging, I nodded reassuringly. They got ready and I called Production to start pumping, with just enough flow to cool the pipe from the heat of welding. They struck blindingly fiery arcs with their welding rods. The next few moments were tense. The relief when it was all over! Relief that had me gulping some cold beers when I shared the experience at home with Pam.

I later attended a fire drill, putting out a real oil fire, where I learned that most grades of crude oil have a high flash point. A lit cigar thrown there didn't ignite it. A welding arc though? Suffice to say, I'm glad not to have been in that particular position ever again.

Pam and I found some oddities in the months that followed; one of which was in the way Nigerians were regarded. It was expressed to us in this way: 'What's the difference between a new arrival and an expat of long standing? Six weeks.' On the surface this was an affront, reminiscent of the bitchy way girls can come across about less fortunate schoolmates, in this case suggesting how those serving us were looked down upon. Some might have meant it that way. More kindly considered the joke was more, out of exasperation, about making allowances for their ignorance and their breaking or losing things. There was a high instance of that. At that time the population was not as highly educated and, more significantly, they had not yet caught up with the fineries of a modern western life style. All of that has changed, with the oil wealth in the east of Nigeria as I'm led to believe in articles.

In that connection, I've noticed something interesting. It was customary for expats to speak with Nigerians in Pidgin English. By contrast, my much more recent experience in South Africa is that Boers persist in English even when spoken to in Pidgin. To us, in Nigeria, Pidgin was more engaging but also more effective as a communication. Perhaps Boers believe in coaxing better use of English or in bringing the dialogue up to their linguistic level?

This was altogether a very new environment for us. Though not so much for me, having lived in Kuwait and in the Lebanon and having visited the West Indies and many other destinations. New to both of us in getting to know some camp wives, though, was that most of them had never set foot outside Umukoroshe except to fly out on their annual vacation; and most of the others merely went on shopping trips into Port Harcourt or to Nigerian markets on the outskirts. The camp was well kept and had a full range of amenities from clinic, shops (most essentially with western groceries), restaurant, bar and cinema to golf course, tennis courts and also sports fields for cricket, football and rugby. It also had tight security, which was especially important in the circumstances. Other than that families could take a trip by company launch, to a secluded beach near the coast.

Beyond the camp old taxis and minibuses jostled with rundown buses that had horrible suspensions and moved crab-like along unlit roads, bumped over ragged potholed verges and barely encountered any traffic lights let alone pedestrian crossings. The best of those roads were maintained by Shell-BP to move heavy equipment along and many others were mere tracks with no ditches to drain rainwater away and keep passers-by from being splashed and drenched.

Trains with steam locomotives over half a century old ran northwards carrying goods to and from the harbour. Trade had been opened up under the British administration for large volume exports – such as palm oil and kernels, tin ore, cocoa and groundnuts – to reach Europe and America as well as for imports – such as salt, bread, flour and soap – to reach the growing population of Nigerians profiting or employed in the export trade.

Buildings were low rise and generally in the washed-out deteriorating state that goes with humid, rainy, stormy conditions. The common areas between buildings showed the neglect that seems to go with urban living pretty much everywhere in the world, even today.

~*~

3   Oh, de bomb not be for you

Finally the crates arrived containing our long awaited wedding gifts, which we had never even seen. That same day I was called to my boss' office for a briefing that I'll never forget.

News that had already been received with relief in the east was that the Military Governor of the Eastern Region, Lieutenant Colonel Odumegwu Ojukwu, had proclaimed the area the Republic of Biafra with secession from Nigeria. Reported on by the local press and evident on the streets, was the joy that hostilities and inequalities would at last end.

That was the previous month. Now, those of us working on pipelines were given the same briefing as in the other offices. Diplomatic efforts at reconciliation had failed. A state of war had been declared and the Nigerian military were taking action.

Foreign governments had advised their nationals to evacuate. Shell was complying with that directive in making arrangements to airlift all staff and their families from Nigeria.

There were repercussions. Shell-BP's Managing Director. Stan Grey, had been detained pending payment of taxes, reparations or whatever from the company. Biafra desperately needed funds for the war effort. Pursuant to that development the company had no option but to keep the semblance of 'operations as usual', in effect that oil was still being produced and exported with income coming in. A select group of volunteers was needed for that purpose. I was volunteered to stay with the group and keep up the pretence of oil operations, well after everyone else in the whole region was evacuated.

I was separately informed that under doctor's advisement, considering Pam's pregnancy, arrangements were instead for her to travel by launch and then by oil tanker.

There was no hysteria, no panic. Everyone got on with arrangements calmly, including my learning to drive a bus should the need arise. I went past a football stadium near the town where a Biafran crowd was being encouraged to come forward as workers in civil defence. We saw early results of that, in roadblocks that caused tailbacks in traffic to and from work. This was tedious but still everyone kept cool, despite the sweltering heat.

An armed soldier in uniform would typically demand, 'Open de boot.' A civil defence worker, a buxom woman with a white tight-fitting tea shirt with 'BIAFRA' printed on the front, would accompany him to the rear of the car. Short on volunteers, outside of people busily making preparations to stay or leave, these civil defence workers were mainly 'ladies of the night'. I first became aware of that when, after casually looking in the boot, one turned to say to me, 'What you dei do tonight?' I smiled politely. She nudged me and blew a kiss, 'You be free, darlen?' Home was just ahead, at the end of the inevitable traffic jam, and that's where I headed!

As in many accounts of cities, when war breaks out, a strange surreal world took over. Everything was there as before and every expectation was that things would somehow be as usual and yet normality was most definitely on hold. It's in such moments that the bizarre can belie a truth. One expat wife went to drive from her house but had to stop because civil defence workers were busily digging across her driveway. She enquired pleasantly enough, 'What you dei do dere?'

'We dig de ditch,' came the answer from smiling lips.

She could see that but had to ask, 'Why?'

'For de bomb.'

OK, she thought, that will be an air raid shelter of sorts, 'Where be my ditch?'

'Oh, de bomb not be for you.'

We weren't involved. Odd, huh? Never mind that we were there, it wasn't our war!

The thousands of evacuees leaving Port Harcourt were allowed just one suitcase aboard the flights arranged for the airlift. All other possessions had to be left behind. Pam and I looked about the house – at clothes and sports gear in cupboards and other things such as a prized sewing machine and, most heart-wrenchingly, at the unopened crate that had arrived. We knew that much of it was from our wedding list at Harrods in London with silver, cut crystal and bone china that we longed to look at and hold. But she'd been advised to put in her case just some food to eat and a change of clothing. She packed a sandwich, a flask of tomato soup and water. We decided to add what couldn't be replaced, photographs, and though hot as she did so she included a coat for UK weather. We comforted ourselves with thinking that we'd be back and we'd have our possessions again. This never happened, all were lost.

That in hand, we made our way to the Port Harcourt harbour; where we said our goodbyes and Pam boarded one of the company's noisy diesel launches for the journey to Shell-BP's Bonny Terminal on the coast. That's where the oil was loaded onto light tankers, for transfer to bigger ones out at sea.

Pam joined 30 or so women, some of whom were pregnant or with young children. There, she clambered up a rope ladder where, nonetheless at just three months old, her bump made it difficult against the vertical hull wall (our baby was a large nine and a half pounder when born).

Always putting on a cheerful face, despite any circumstances, apparently the captain of the oil tanker noticed and kindly gave her his cabin. All of the crew gave up their cabins to the evacuees.

When they reached Fernando Po, the women were taken ashore in another launch, before a manic driver drove them along a winding mountain road to a hotel. Pam had not eaten, she'd been that nauseous and worried about what was happening to me. There were injections for sickness, which other pregnant mothers had, but which Pam declined.

The farcical episode continued the next day, when they found themselves wading on a wet floor in the Dakota they boarded. There was a leak, presumably in the galley. Transferred to another Dakota, some arduous hours later, they then had to endure a very uncomfortable flight, which was both slow and unpressurised, before finally arriving in England. It cannot be overstated how relieved Pam was to be greeted by her parents as well as Shell staff who handed her some expense money (£200).

I was assigned the bungalow and servants of a Dutch family, in Umukoroshe, the aim being to keep us 'volunteers' together there. The family had gone and the father now asked one favour of me, 'When the time comes – there was no conviction in his tone, about the idyllic life in the camp actually ending – will you put down our two cats?'

'Sure.'

'Meanwhile would you look after them? We wash them frequently.'

A bit weird, I thought. But, heck, those were their cats, and now my house mates.

~*~

4 We were hostages

Suddenly all foreign nationals had gone, as had all aircraft and vessels; there were no trains, buses or other means of transport for us, except for our company vehicles. Just 60 of us expat men remained, cut off from the outside world among Biafran soldiers and millions of Biafran civilians. There was no means of communicating with the outside either; among us we used short-range handheld radios. Senior members of the group must have had some contact, to know when we could leave, though possibly that was through the Biafran Army. We were located at the southern most end of Biafra, which occupied roughly the same surface area as Scotland. The rest of Nigeria bordered Biafra to the west and north; and we'd have to reach there in order to get out. The Atlantic Ocean was to the south and Cameroon, which supported Nigeria in the war, bordered Biafra to the east.

All we really knew was that Stan Grey was under house arrest and that he'd been taken to a hotel in the port and market town of Onitsha – a town on the Niger River border with Nigeria that has two old Cathedrals.

We were free to go about our business, which mainly entailed checking on oil facilities and pipelines, but we'd only be free to leave when the payment demanded of Shell-BP had been paid and

Stan Grey released. As far as we knew Ojukwu had kept the dealings and negotiations with Shell-BP civil, as the Biafran Army more-or-less was with us. Nevertheless, restrained as we all were, payment was now effectively the ransom for our release. And that pretty well meant that we were all hostages.

At 23, probably the youngest there, I guess my composure came from the sense the others had that this would soon blow over. More than that though, from the moment Pam and I had arrived in the region I had never felt any hostility toward us. To the contrary there was, for want of anything else to describe it, the sort of regard that good pupils have for their teacher. We also meant employment. Nevertheless being new to Africa, as a working adult, I couldn't help but look out from the open-sided clubhouse and scan the sports fields every now and then as we watched movies at night. Not that I knew what to do if I saw Nigerian troops, federal troops as they were soon called, approaching across the grass.

The only news we could get of the outside world was from BBC radio. Most of all, we hoped to hear what was happening all around us with the war. Were the federals advancing, towards us?

It transpires that London was probably as much in the dark as us. The Nigerian Air Force was built to West German Luftwaffe standards with the help of 26 of their advisors; all of whom left at this time, after one was killed in a B-26 bombing raid on Kaduna air base. We'd heard of the six-day war between Egypt and Israel, with the Soviet involvement in that, but I had no idea of the Czechoslovak involvement in Nigeria. Their Air Force delivered bombs, rockets and eight L-29 Delfin training aircraft in the first month of the war, which soon bombed the Biafran airfield in Uli and areas with large concentrations of civilians.

Tension! Mind-blowing tension! Which called for mind-blowing diversion, or sheer fun. I connected with a young colleague, George Hornby, in nightly drinking sessions. So much so, that one evening George stopped his car by the roadside in the camp and got out. He was found the next morning sleeping like a baby at the bottom of a large storm ditch he had dropped into.

He related an amusing thing one day. Each morning on walking past his African Grey parrot, nursing a hangover, he'd been greeted with screeches as if the bird was laughing at him. So, that last evening to get his own back he had put a few drops of gin in the parrot's water. In the morning he expected to laugh at the parrot's hangover. Instead, he was horrified to see the bird lying lifeless with feet up in the cage. His horror dissolved into the anticipated laughter when he heard a low pitched groan and saw one eyelid half open to direct a pained stare at him. The bird never laughed at him again!

I told him about a holiday we'd had in Malta and he recalled a time spent there when Mickey Rooney was sitting at a table near to him. George was not tall and stood up smoking a cigar. At that Mickey got off his chair, standing no taller than he was seated, and called over, 'I used to smoke those. But they stunted my growth.' George was a Geordie, possessing their wicked sense of humour.

Apart from fooling around there wasn't anything productive for me to do. My activity simply involved showing up around the offices and materials yard. Some of the others, however, drove out to the oilfields where, thankfully, they did not find any leaks or, worse still, fires for which they were on the look out.

They did see federal troops though and their movements told us far more than the radio divulged. One guy scoffed, in the dark way of relieving tension, when recounting about villagers slaughtered in the crossfire of combatants, which left all of us feeling deeply for the civilians. The derision was for the troops who skirted around in opposite directions so as not to risk engaging with each other directly.

The dearth of reliable news, unsettling in itself, appeared to have sparked some unprofessionalism in the international press; which could be exemplified by this from a diplomatic correspondent for the Financial Times: Northerners might "*already have begun to take revenge for the death of their leader the Sardauna of Sokoto on the large number of Igbo who live in the North*". With nothing of the sort having taken place the report, from a highly respected journal, could possibly have inflamed already heightened tensions and even led the

Northern elite to the very massacre it seems to have prophesised – the massacre that led to war.

This disconnect, of the modern Western psyche, was in not recognising that Africans would be among the readers and that they would take in their words faithfully. A disconnect that I fear lives on still.

It turns out that the federals had denied reporters any access to the new republic of Biafra; which explains why we at the receiving end were so misinformed. We really were in the dark. Instead, we had to rely on our own observations.

An incident, we talked about, was remarkable in illustrating the extraordinary regard the local people had for us – and, in my experience, I'd extend that regard further across rural Nigeria and even Africa. One of our guys visiting the Oguta oilfield in a Land Rover, hit a mine with such force that the explosion shot the engine right through the chassis. Others saw the wrecked vehicle when they went there the following day. The man, luckily as it happens, was blasted into the adjoining field where a local farmer was tending his crops. Though likely in shock himself, the Igbo put the severely injured body across his bicycle and rode over 40 km to the Biafran barracks in Owerri.

Igbo troops then put our man in a jeep and drove over 90 km through the night to reach our doctor's house in Umukoroshe. They got the doctor's attention but not before pounding on the door and getting ready to break it in, the soldiers were that intent on getting the injured man seen to.

One could envisage war, the hatred and carnage there'd been, and perhaps a rebelliousness in having broken from Nigeria, to have soured attitudes toward us – a small band of expats that were left behind. As this incident showed, nothing could be further from the reality of our existence there. Nothing had changed; I'd go further and say nothing had changed since colonial times. We were, as then, well regarded. It made this ordeal bearable in that I was readily looked after by stewards in the camp; and I was comfortably cared for in the bungalow.

The only thing that was onerous, was my having to face washing the cats, as promised. This was new to me, having always had dogs in my life. I spied a basin in the garden, which seemed the most likely place for the deed and, turning a tap, let the basin fill a bit. One cat was ginger, the other black and white. Whichever I picked up and lifted to the water exploded with hisses, screeches and flaying claws that also splashed scalding *hot water* on me. The servants hardly hid their giggles. Hot water? I'd turned the wrong tap! But then, a hot water tap installed in a garden? This took me completely by surprise.

Finally the time came when we could leave and my first thought went, most reluctantly, to honouring my pledge about the cats. The concern for life witnessed in the Oguta event was not extended to animals. The cats had no chance of surviving on their own. It was commonly held, of local attitudes towards animals: If it moves kill it; afterwards think about whether it's edible.

I put the cats in the back of the second hand Renault we'd bought, unthinkingly as it turns out. Perhaps the purr of the engine was not their purr; or maybe they'd never been in a vehicle in motion before. Or the one I scalded might have turned maniacal. Whatever the reason, I had reached the outskirts of Port Harcourt when suddenly they bolted over the passenger seat, screeched and ran amuck clawing at the upholstery. I had to continue. All about were signs of an evacuation reminiscent of the quasi colonial *Gone With The Wind*: empty premises, vehicles parked in disarray being loaded with possessions, Biafran crowds hastening about. One of the cats slashed at my trouser, drawing blood. With one hand I hurled it to the back while struggling to steer. I was driving slowly, while peering to see the vet's house. Again, there was a complete absence of hostility or none that I felt. A pungent smell filled the air, though, and I saw that they'd both shat and pissed on the seats. The house was abandoned, the vet gone. I returned, rubbing my wounded leg, to Umukoroshe. On the way back, it seems strange now, the cats were quieter. Perhaps it was some aura in the town that had spooked them. The only recourse I had was to call Dr. Ben Van Haften, who put each cat in a shoebox and chloroformed it. I then watched as he buried them in the garden.

The next evening we all congregated at one of the houses, to celebrate our departure. But, with all of us merry on beer, it was horribly sobering when Bob Boyson arrived from a field trip. Though unhurt himself his car was riddled with bullet holes.

This was in stark contrast to the experience one guy had earlier, which we'd all laughed at. He'd come back from walking along a pipeline trace where he'd caught sight of troops coming out of the woods some ways ahead of him. They, certainly federals he thought, opened fire. 'It was OK', he reported. 'They were aiming at me!'

~*~

5 We got into wooden canoes and paddled hard

The next day we set off in a convoy of 20 cars, travelling 180 km on empty roads with no federal troops sighted and only an agonising number of Biafran roadblocks to worry about. I worried needlessly that word of our convey coming through might not have reached them. All were exasperatingly slow in letting us pass but none turned out to be a problem, presumably because of our Biafran escorts. We arrived in Onitsha at dusk and went straight to the Niger River. I was gaining huge confidence in Shell-BP's organisational abilities, in this tricky situation; but the light was fading fast and we had the river to cross, under the guns of federal troops on the far bank as well as up above on the far side of the fairly recently built Niger Bridge.

In the end Ojukwu was good to his word. Stan Grey was freed. One million pounds sterling had been handed over, when a Barclays Bank official reached there with a suitcase full of the cash, and we were all free to leave. With no further ado we all got into wooden canoes and paddled hard to get away, making headway as far as we could upstream of the bridge. In the enveloping darkness we worried about federal troops mistaking our silhouettes for the invading enemy – but not far from the bank we had other worries. We were taking in water and near to sinking. Fortunately a quick thinking engineer pulled his jacket over the bow and under the leak. That just did the trick, we reached the far side.

I learnt several months later that, just days after our escape, the Biafran Army crossed the Niger Bridge to invade the Midwest state of Nigeria that we were now entering.

Cars were awaiting us on the far bank and we set off again in convoy for the 160 km journey to Ughelli. Now in full darkness, happily encountering no roadblocks, or perhaps I dozed through them, we were only stopped by a herd of cows blocking the narrow road. Any delay was troubling, though, and getting 20 cars through was an agony. Finally we arrived at our destination, Shell-BP's Ughelli production centre.

We now had refreshments and a chance to rest, while awaiting our airlift to Lagos in the morning. Others had arrived, including an Irish priest who reeled on while downing more beer. 'I don't know,' he bowed and shook his head. 'I've lived among these people for 25 years; and now I see they're savages.' Whatever everyone's experiences were, some could have been decidedly traumatic. I never heard what he had seen.

The Shell doctor, for the Ughelli area, was a lot more forthcoming about the events of the last couple of days. He recounted to a couple of us that a young American girl, who had been working with a village for the American Peace Corps, had come to him the day before requesting an examination. At first reticent, he acceded to the request when she told him of the premarital circumcision, a public ceremony, her Nigerian fiancée had talked her into. Despite the crude cuts involving an old razor blade, the doctor found nothing untoward.

The reason for the doctor unloading all of this to us now was that the girl had returned, that morning, in a terrible state. Crying and sobbing she'd told of the fiancée having fled with her purse, all her money and her passport. She was destitute. The doctor reasoned how this had come about: that she'd lost the boy's respect by coming down to his level. The doctor grieved over what would become of the girl but was unable to help. He too was being airlifted out. All expats were, save for the girl of whom we heard nothing more.

~*~

6 *You leave next week*

Pam and I related much of our experiences to her mother Violet and grandmother Amy; the latter was in her eighties and appeared more preoccupied with the canary in a cage next to her when we visited them in Surbiton, Surrey, UK. She seemed to listen and then gave the strangest of responses, 'That's nice, dear. And, did the milkman visit every day?' That was customary in most homes of the day in Britain but was, of course, unheard of in the wilds of Nigeria and ridiculous in the context of wartime evacuations anywhere.

Pam, with some assistance from Shell, had rented a flat not far away. But, with leave given to recuperate, we set off to England's Lake District in the sunshine of a pleasant summer. We had beauty at last, and scenery with gentle hills and trees, which we stared at from a boat we rowed aimlessly on the lake. To our surprise we'd not been there long, or it didn't seem we had, when I had a phone call telling me to report to Shell-BP in The Hague, Holland.

The company had temporary offices in Scheveningen, on the sea near to The Hague, above a nightclub; where it tickled us guys that some girls from the club brought us coffee – huh, the rest was only in our imaginations. We quickly got apartments for our wives to join us. I accompanied Pam for prenatal visits to a doctor who advised us of priorities at the hospital, which attended to Queen Juliana, where we'd booked to have the birth. He advised us that in the event of a complication, it being a catholic facility, they would save the child. OK, noted! I was there, as we wished anyway, throughout the long 24-hour labour; I was ready to ensure nothing of the sort would happen.

In later years I was always the brunt of snide jokes, about my having gone back to sleep when her labour pains started in the night. It was only because I'd thought it best to be on the ball at the hospital.

We'd asked the doctor not to tell us whether a boy or a girl would soon join us. Scans were becoming available but we preferred to be surprised. That made the task of choosing a name doubly difficult and despite reading up on the choices we'd failed to settle on any. Except, in that moment of Pam pacing about with labour pains and me going back to sleep, I dreamed of the names Natasha and Denise. I woke and told Pam, who beamed back immediately, 'Yes. Yes, that's good.' We went to the hospital with no other names in mind and strangely with no inclination to have a boy's name ready.

Delivery of the nine and a half pound parcel was mercilessly excruciating for Pam. The Catholic hospital did not permit the use of gas or other painkillers. When that adorable girl arrived and cried Pam was at last able to see and hear the miracle she'd brought into the world. We both were.

The greatest of anything we'd ever accomplished was right there.

We had some time together as a family, in which we enjoyed taking Natasha to parties and showing off how quiet and happy she was. We also treated ourselves to the latest in hi-fi equipment, with the delight of listening to 60's music with superb acoustic quality.

Then unexpectedly, for we had no idea what to expect, my Dutch boss, Ron Timmerman, announced for all to hear in the office that they'd received a telex from Lagos, following the return of a first batch of engineers. It read, 'Delicious! Send more!' He then turned to me, 'You leave, next week.' I was to go back.

There was never any discussion. That was it. The view was: I look after the company and it looks after me. As it all turned out it worked, they were good to me and my family.

It was left to Pam, there being no time to do otherwise, to pack up our home and, with baby Natasha, go by ferry to the UK. She rented a flat in Walton-upon-Thames, Surrey.

~*~

Midwest Nigeria

7 A gélè, expressed everything

I had a caravan at the Ughelli production centre, the scene of such mayhem when airlifted out just months earlier. The location was some distance from where the main office would be, in Warri, but closest to my work among the oilfields. I'd arrived as part of a small team, half a dozen engineers, ahead of the full mobilisation of scores. Even specialist inspectors who would check the integrity of construction works were yet to arrive. We were alone save for a doctor to tend our needs, and those who secured the basics for our use, such as vehicles, accommodation and communications.

Of course there were the local people in each village. Unlike Port Harcourt this was not a densely populated area; the only two storey buildings were in Warri. Yes, we were amused – okay, mostly we weren't – by finding military roadblocks a common feature when travelling around.

I learnt, around that time, that the Biafran Army had gone through there, en route to capture Lagos – somewhere on that road a wrecked tank had stood as a symbol of the battles – and had been driven back across the Niger Bridge a matter of days later. That took place some six months earlier and I was conscious that the bridge, the front line, was just a short drive away.

I've since appreciated the significance of the Prague Spring, which occurred around this time, in that it was a period of political liberalisation in Czechoslovakia when restrictions on the media were loosened. Articles questioning the deliveries of armaments to Nigeria appeared in their national press and in response to public opinion the supplies were stopped. Shortly after, however, the Soviets invaded Czechoslovakia and the embargo was lifted – for the express purpose of re-orientating Nigeria to the Soviet Block, which never happened. Supplies were routed via Egypt and Egyptian pilots were conscripted to fly missions for the Nigerian Air Force.

Oblivious of such developments, we had to have the odd laugh to preserve our sanity. Federal troops were apt to stop us, at gunpoint, for a lift. With the menacing look I got from one, I let him climb into the back seat and alight when we reached Warri. I was only too ready to make my getaway but was startled, on reaching the office and parking my Peugeot, to see a hand grenade where he'd sat.

I had the contractors for constructing an assortment of main and minor pipelines under my charge; and, despite being thin on the ground, we had to push hard to get the lines built while the dry season lasted. Oil production had halted in the intervening months and we had to get it back on stream.

Naturally enough, relationships were edgy. I was challenged, almost at the outset, when a contractor asked for instructions. A valve, of a totally new design (a ball valve), had to be welded into the

38

pipeline and they wanted to be sure about the welding procedure. I had no idea about that, but thought I knew a man who did.

I shot off down the road, through roadblocks, to Warri, where I went straight to see my Australian boss, Dave Gerber. I knocked at his door, pushed ahead while turning the handle, and my face banged the unrelenting door, before I realised that this handle had to be turned *up* instead of down. A carpenter had relocated the door, upside down. Composure a little dented, for that first meeting with my boss, I forged ahead. His response to hearing about the valve problem was brief, 'That's what you're here for'.

'Oh', I thought.

Composure still intact, I went for a pee in a toilet with an open window and a surprising view, as if from a theatre box, over a muddy abattoir. Before me to gaze at, hopefully not the other way round in my state of undress, was a corner of a local market where stalls were busy with shoppers – ladies topped by vivid head-ties and wearing full-length wraps that trailed over the mud and men with shirts and their wraps.

I understand that oil wealth has transformed eastern Nigerians, who now have cars, TVs and trendy globalised fashions. Back then though, the brilliant colours the Nigerians could have in wraps, not brash but elegant, appealed to me. Distinction, individuality and creativity were essential fashion statements. The material said a lot about social status; cloth had been made in some regions and imported across the Sahara long before it was brought in by European traders. For a very long time materials were the currency of West Africa; the equivalent of five yards would buy a bull or go towards the dowry for a bride and some was kept in pristine condition to maintain the value.

Of all wraps the head-tie, known as a gélè, expressed everything about the women; the quality of cloth naturally spoke of their station and sophistication, how they shaped it eluded to how imaginative or moody they felt that day, and if so inclined they'd even signal their marital status in the way the tips were pointing. The gélè's practicality came in when used to carry a heavy basket or even a log, which the women did as they walked with the incredible balance and stance of a ballerina.

My water flowed just as one of the cows, so skinny its ribs showed, had a machete drawn across its neck. The animal flopped to the ground under the apparently detached gaze of equally skinny cows. You'd think they'd run or panic, not just stand there.

Just then a young Nigerian girl blocked the view, standing right in front of me. Tray in hand she was on the balcony that ran outside, colonial style, the length of the building. Eyes on me, with no head-tie and wearing a simple skirt-length wrap, she asked with a sweet smile, 'You dei wan tea?' She didn't look down (or I don't think she did) nor did she blush. I didn't, either.

Yes, I'd been in the country long enough to make out features on very black faces. As nonchalantly as I could put my member back in my trousers, watching amazed at her and the poor cows and the crowd beyond, I answered softly but assertively, 'Yes, thank you.'

A vision of another sort happened when I took a canoe across a river to check on preparations on the far bank. Lengths of pipe were welded together. Soon they'd be joined, coated in asphalt and concrete, floated and then sunk across the river. There was smoke from a fire and ladies with head-ties and colourful full-length wraps were preparing food for the locally hired pipeline gang (all Nigerians, of course).

Banana leaves were placed on the large pipes with bits of meat on them. Curious, for some bits didn't register as anything I'd come across before, I stepped forward and faltered for an instant at the sight of tiny *seared fingers*. I had to peer hard to be sure and, yes, that's definitely what they were. The urge unsatiated I simply couldn't ask, and thereby imply otherwise, whether those were monkey bits. Dark visions, of other possibilities, I quickly dispelled with a shudder.

There was no doubting that this terrain was wild and, in that respect, perhaps one particular moment served to temper relations with one contractor. I was the 'enemy' one could say – I never felt nor encouraged that perception – in between contractors and the few inspectors we now had.

I was standing alongside Steve Masri, contract manager for some main lines that the Lebanese contractor Mothercat was building, when a small green snake landed from a branch high above and slipped off my shoulder. I'd just watched an inspector torture a snake that had fallen in the pipeline ditch, by putting to its tail the 10,000 volt wand they used to check pipe coatings. They laughed as the snake 'zinged' out 'straight as an arrow'. I looked at Steve and he at me, as our green snake slithered away, neither of us thinking about the antics of the construction crew. We both moved on.

I did follow up on that though, in discussion with our doctor, 'Our cars won't be kitted out with anti-venom serum, as they were before war broke out?'

'No, that was just as dangerous if administered inadvertently. Actually there are 2,400 species of snake in Africa and only 800 are poisonous.'

'Oh.' I wasn't in the least reassured by those figures – by the one in three chance of being fatally bitten. 'So, what should I do if bitten?'

'First look to see how many bite holes you have. If there are two, they were where the venom was injected; otherwise you have nothing to worry about.'

'OK, what then?'

'You have to remain calm. Don't do anything to get your blood, with the venom in it, racing. And get to a clinic as fast as you can.'

'Ahuh,' I thought, 'Be calm and yet rush there? Neat!' Much of my time was spent deep in the forests, where snakes were really not that uncommon, and seriously far from any clinic.

Another disquieting moment occurred when driving to Warri one day. On approaching a small village I noticed an oldish man, barely clad, crawling along the verge just short of the first huts. I was sure he'd be helped by villagers; not that my stopping to help was encouraged. Quite the opposite, it was strongly discouraged. The belief held was that by getting involved, the person helped would forever pester for hand-outs.

On my return, I kept an eye out for him and saw a prostrate body as I approached the far end of the village. He'd crawled right past all the huts, and people milling about, and died alone. I reflected on how different the Igbo had been toward our man injured by a land mine near Oguta. The difference wasn't that of Igbo versus Yoruba. We expats mattered to them all, more than their own – what else were we there for, other than as employers – or more than those from other villages or tribes.

I reflected on that indifference to others, I'd witnessed. That uncaring trait conjured up images of Europe's industrial era and well before that time too; when there'd been a detachment bordering on hostility to any newcomer, whether from another village or with a different accent, let alone from a different tribe with another tongue altogether.

Aside from war and starvation that killed tens of millions across Eurasia, exemplifying the worst of those times among ordinary people: the coasts of Cornwall, in Britain, were thought to be where 'wreckers' built bonfires, resembling lighthouse beacons, to lure vessels onto rocks. *Cornish Wrecking 1700-1860* by Kathryn J. Pearce has dispelled that cruellest of activities as a myth, though not the part that local people played in plundering the possessions of shipwreck victims. The majority were not murderers, but rather regarded any foreigners callously, and opportunistically so. In the main, the same must be said of plantation owners who bought and sold slaves like merchandise, and men the world over who still treat women as property. Further examples were landowners and industrialists, who put children to work in fields, factories and mines. Not all acted cruelly but certainly callously by modern European standards.

Those archaic attitudes, belonging to ancient or medieval times, have died hard. West Africa was no exception with chiefs selling captives of tribal raids – for over a millennia into the trans-Saharan slave trade from Kano, northern Nigeria, then into the trans-Atlantic slave trade to the New World, and later eastward to Asia. These routes were used in trafficking slaves, through the bloody unification of Britain under the Stuarts and through the carnage of the English civil war as well as the American War of

Independence, the French Revolution and the start of the Napoleonic Wars.

Such was the prevalence of war and conquest and yet, spurred on by slave revolts in the West Indies, William Wilberforce and supporters put the abolition of slavery into the law of the world's superpower of the day – Britain. It's strange to think that humanitarian reforms at home came later – such as the emancipation of women, the abolition of child labour and the end to sending convicts (much like slaves) to penal colonies in Australia – reforms inspired by, among others, English writer Charles Dickens (who incidentally was only born just after Wilberforce's act).

The West Africa Squadron of the Royal Navy, the largest fleet in the world following Britain's victory in the Napoleonic Wars, used force as well as treaties to abolish slave trafficking on the high seas – effectively quashing that trade to the Americas – while, most significantly, the British West Africa administration enforced the abolition throughout Nigeria.

That said, such battles are never over; the UN estimates there are upwards of 21 million people living in slavery, worldwide, today. Added to that there is piracy off the coasts of West Africa, as well as in mainland Nigeria, where the fight against Boko Haram, recently allied with Islamic State, has continued for six years, to date, and seen thousands taken as slaves and thousands more slaughtered.

There are attitudes, archaic uncaring attitudes, that fester in our midst and have no place in the modern *social* world. Those attitudes must surely go now.

~*~

8 SHELL ENGINEER YOU GO PASS DIS PLACE YOU GO DIE O

Masri and I got on reasonably well, while I never let up on what needed to be done. So it was gratifying when he called me by radio one day, 'George, you must come! Right away!' He gave me the location and, prompted by the urgency in his tone, I sped round immediately. He was standing where bulldozers had pushed through the forest to clear a trace for a main line. I knew where that progress had reached. All activity had stopped. All machines were shut down and everyone was also standing about.

Masri pointed to the wall of trees that were to have come down, but where planks had instead been nailed across the trunks to make a crude notice board. In red were written the words: SHELL ENGINEER YOU GO PASS DIS PLACE YOU GO DIE O. Steve leaned my way, 'You see? I don't want you to go die o.' I had to laugh with him, but I also knew to take this seriously. Delays of this sort were intolerable in the tight schedule and they cost dearly in contractual claims. I sped to Warri, straight to the Legal office of Shell-BP.

The outcome was incredible. The contractor was to redeploy his workforce. After consultation with the Ministry of Mines and Power, Shell-BP received special dispensation to reroute the line around that forest. This was unheard of. Pipeline licenses took months to be approved and this small detour was approved in just days. The forest was not to be messed with.

In this connection, several months later I learned something disturbingly sinister. I'd gone to the manager of NEPA (National Electric Power Authority) in Warri for permission to open a road so that we could cross a pipeline under it. Cables were in the road and they needed to be protected. He was a large man wearing a navy suit, Yoruba I imagined him, although possibly Edo or Ijaw, seated at an equally large desk, in a large office, with a pile of envelopes on it. I was accustomed to starting any conversation with a bit of convivial chat but he neither paid attention to the purpose of my visit nor anything else. His mind was wandering along lines I couldn't begin to guess at.

'You see these envelopes? You know what they are?' I shrugged and said that I didn't. 'They are pay cheques,' his expression demanded comprehension, which I couldn't give, 'for staff who died. My staff.' He might as well have been TV quiz presenter Stephen Fry, I was so lost in this discourse, asking me a quirky question. 'Do you know how many died? How many the Biafrans killed, when they came through?' I hadn't even known, just then, that they had. 'They bulldozed open a grave and shoved in masses of bodies.'

The Biafrans had invaded and been driven back by the federals the previous year. Reports on actual events started to appear in the foreign press later than the on-the-spot reports I was hearing. They told of more atrocities, with thousands killed, perpetrated by both Biafran and federal armies as well as of reprisals against Igbo resistance units active during the invasion of the Midwest.

There was a long pause, with me unable to offer anything in response, I was that wrapped up in construction pressures and blind to anything else. I remained so, all the time I was in the area. He carried on regardless, 'I saw a boy by the road, not anyone I knew. When I came back his body was there, on the ground, where I'd seen him standing before.'

I was totally unprepared for anything like this, unaware of any of these events. I doubt any of us could have been otherwise, and now, looking back, I was unprepared to even be the good listener the man, whom I presumed to be an engineer like myself, so desperately wanted.

Well, perhaps in part that's not true. I sat there, knowing only that to say anything would have been trite. I had neither wisdom nor solace to offer on any of this; and so, I listened. 'We've lost so many, and so many young ones.'

He had to continue, and I had to hear. But as he did so, he hit me as if with Thor's hammer. 'There is a forest near Ughelli, where they practice juju. They sit in a circle, cut off the head of a chicken and swing it round so that its blood goes to everyone.' I knew juju was commonly practiced. I'd seen the burial sites, where the dead were placed on a platform of branches up a tree and left for nature's 'spirits' to take the body away. Even so, his depiction seemed straight out of a B-grade horror movie.

What came next nailed me to my chair. Without any malice or shouting, he went on, 'No! They were not chickens! No... babies!' This man's outpourings were straight out of hell. 'Five hundred babies. Five hundred... went missing last year.' That was the year of the invasion.

I've come across nothing written of such juju rites, perpetrated in Ughelli or wherever. Is it conceivable that the atrocities of war had elicited such a horrendous response among the worshippers? Perhaps what was convincing, for me, was this man's calm sincerity in the face of so much trauma.

Whatever the truth, I have never forgotten that meeting – a grizzly echo of Joseph Conrad's *Heart of Darkness*, the inspiration for Francis Coppola's movie *Apocalypse Now*, played out fully in real life – and the Ughelli forest with the *bloody* message to me, which by Government authority had been detoured so readily.

~*~

9   *Dere be people hurt here!*

That meeting with the NEPA manager took place weeks later. For now pressure mounted to get the pipelines finished – and the specialist inspectors were finally all on hand to check what they could of the work done. Much of the pipe had already been buried. Minor lines were not for burying anyway and one very long line was found to have defective welding. The welders had missed out the root and bead welds and simply put the cap welds in place. Of course, it would have failed the hydrostatic testing to which we subjected all completed lines.

Remedial works would have cost the small Lebanese contractor dearly and management wanted to keep the select band of contractors in this conflict zone fully engaged, so that it was instead agreed to pay for the repairs.

We had our pressures too, with inspectors nervous about roadblocks and such; and I was pushing them, quite possibly too hard, for rigorous inspection whilst also speedy progress. It's also possible that I'd been conditioned beyond empathy by my experiences in Port Harcourt.

War was somewhere not far away and it didn't help that news of it was at best patchy, while most often blatantly questionable. The federal ban on foreign reporters going to Biafra had attracted armchair journalists accommodated at the Federal

51

Palace Hotel, Victoria Island, Lagos. Also staying there or visiting the bar there were Nigerian Air Force mercenaries – who were mostly Egyptian, with one or two South African, an Australian and an English pilot among them – from whom they got snippets of whatever, having overflown villages and towns.

A rude reminder of the pressure everyone felt occurred when playing darts one evening at our bar. I'd gone to retrieve my darts from the board, when another slammed in between my thumb and index finger, thrown there with all the force the man could have propelled it. I turned to see the senior inspector's face red with anger or whatever. Nothing was said and I left. Nothing more was ever said and there was no recurrence. Possibly they all knew these were exceptional circumstances, war is never kind – we heard of guys in Warri who'd turned to drink, spending their evenings cowered under tables out of fear – or, maybe, I never played darts with them again?

That pressure was there on the day a completed main line, a vital link for opening production, was being hydrostatically tested. It was a lengthy process, filling many miles of the large pipe and building pressure, and my radio crackled with the voice of a senior inspector, 'It's failed!' The line had burst, somewhere, and we had to find out where. I dreaded that being in a river crossing, the hardest of all places to locate a break.

My mind raced with the possibilities as I drove on roads in the general direction of the line, and as I probably took a sharp bend in the road a little too widely. BAM!

Suddenly a voice was calling out, 'Oh, sorry masta! Sorry!' I followed the direction from which it came, my eyes struggling to focus, and found a strained black smile beaming back. The poor man was kneeling to view me, across the underneath of my car, while I, still seated, viewed him with my head dangling down through the open driver's door. Yet he, the driver of a monster Mack oilfield truck, was concerned about me? Or about my reaction? And that was it, Oh, sorry masta? The large pipe for a bumper had flattened my bonnet, demolished the windscreen, removed the whole of the roof and severed the top of my seat. I'd have been decapitated had I been wearing a seat belt.

That's what staff in the Warri office thought when they recognised my crushed Peugeot being towed past their windows. They weren't to know how hell bent I was to get the pipeline sorted.

Following a cursory check up by the Shell doctor in Ughelli, and with fragments of glass removed, I secured another vehicle and carried on. There was nothing else for me there, but to keep busy.

I had another disastrous moment, the tension of hydrostatically testing yet another pipeline on my mind, when I drove round a sharp bend in the road from Ughelli to Warri. This time I slammed into a frenzied crowd who shouted and screamed. A blur of orange, red, black and yellow whisked all about as they in their wraps swarmed with hands and fists slamming frantically on bonnet, roof and windows. I'd braked in time, and they'd parted too, not to hit any of the men and women, but now I could not move forward or back. I was trapped in a din that made it hard to think.

It took a moment for me to make out a bus on its side by the road and a minibus in a ditch. They were shrieking at me, incoherently, and all my instincts were also yelling at me, 'They want my car! Why? They want my car!' Yet, what they were not doing was rocking the car or pulling open doors or breaking windows. I quickly resolved, 'Whatever they want of my car, I must remain with it.' I could not be left stranded out there in their midst. I opened the front passenger window so that no blows could reach me, and mustered as much authority as I could towards the man nearest to the car. That's when he shouted, 'Dere be people hurt here! Badly hurt people!'

'OK. OK.' I replied, while the imperative that shaped in my thoughts differed, 'They have to get them to a hospital, in this car, but,' I resolved, 'with me in charge and with no frantic passengers. I told the man, 'I take two injured. No one else.'

To my astonishment the shouting abated, doors opened, and they carefully laid a man in a dirty wrap across the back seat and rested his badly bleeding foot there. I remained firmly in my seat. In the front they seated a man, also in a dirty wrap, whose arm had been broken and was twisted round at his back. They all stood back and I eased the car forward. Yet, though I watched their faces as they let me get clear, my thoughts were still on my own safety and not for an instant on the trust they were putting in this white stranger. Only later would I learn how very important these charges were and, now, I have to reflect, 'Who was I to be trusted so?'

I sped off. The journey took about 30 minutes, remarkably with no holdup at the one roadblock encountered; and however I found the way, perhaps the man in the front helped, I got us to the local Warri clinic and parked as close as I could to the one story building. There was a deep storm ditch in between, with a bridge that male and female nurses in white tunics came over. They put a canvas stretcher on the gravel and very indelicately, I thought, plopped the man from the back seat down onto it. I guess his pain masked the hurt of landing on the lumpy hard ground. Once inside, with both men placed in beds and covered with white sheets, I made to leave. Except, some sense of responsibility tugged at my conscience. I had to ask, 'What happens now? Some formality, anything?'

'Oh, they be in good hands.' Whatever demeanour the female nurse had, I guess it didn't exactly convince when she said, 'You can go now.'

'Nothing to sign?'

'No, you dei go now.'

I made to go. Except, I had to know, 'Is the doctor coming?'

'He be at home, on de break. He deal wid dem when he come back.' She insisted, 'You dei go now.'

No, wrong answer, that wasn't good enough. It was time to be assertive, as Pam had on occasion commented I should be; I'd simply been disinclined that way, overtly, and now it was a necessity. 'What's his address?' I wasn't taking 'No' for an answer and finally got to where he lived. I knocked at his door. An Indian man in a suit, the doctor for sure, opened it and I went straight to the matter, 'I just left two men, injured in a collision on the road, at your clinic. One is bleeding badly.'

He answered eloquently, also very assuredly, 'That's fine, I'll attend to them presently. You can go now.'

'He's bleeding badly.'

'I'll just finish my lunch and then be along.'

I just stared, incredulously and yet angrily too I guess, for that's what I felt. I'd said all that was to be said and held my ground. That seemed to do the trick. The doctor got in his car and I followed. He stood at the man's bed and reiterated, 'OK, we'll take it from here.'

'But, what will you do?' Perhaps I'd become accustomed to taking charge of things, and though this was out of my league I had to see it through.

If he had any discomfort with what he next said, I wasn't aware of it, 'If I were in the UK, where I had my training, we'd try to save his foot. But...' By inference, they would not. Reluctantly, I left it at that. The doctor had given me his time, followed at my request, and, it seems to me now, he too had deferred to my authority.

I guess too, I must have stared incredulously again. Some months later, now deskbound with an office in Warri, I was called by our receptionist. She gave the name of a chief who wanted to see me and I said that was okay, though having no idea who the man might be. Lots of chiefs had contracts providing work for their villagers. But this man, dressed magnificently in fine colourful wraps and wearing a hat befitting a Yoruba chief, surprised me as he came through my door and sat down. He wasn't there for any other purpose, having taken the time to dress so ceremoniously and come there specially, than to thank me for saving his foot.

Everyone was advised of the repercussions that were likely to arise by stopping or getting involved in incidents. This was a wild country and a chilling reminder of that happened when I was much later working in Lagos. An American mother decided to avoid heavy traffic and told her driver to go through the outskirts to get her eight year old daughter to school on time. In one of the villages a child ran in front of their car. The woman instinctively slammed the back of the driver's seat, 'Stop!' He reacted instantly as ordered but also fled from the car. The door next to the daughter was flung open. Gripped in shock, the mother watched helplessly as villagers dragged the girl by her blond hair and beheaded her. It was over that quickly.

The fine chief of my experience was not like anyone in the many warnings we had received. I'd not been in danger, nor was he intent on hanging on to me for support; nor was he, I feel sure as he never came back again, about getting contracts. Rather, his visit was simply to return respect, chief to engineer; which I regret maybe not having acknowledged well enough or magnanimously enough, my head still buzzing over pipes, at the time.

10 We sensed no hostility

Not long after the bus collision incident I had a knock on the door of my caravan and opened it to see two barely clad black traders. I was used to that. They'd arrive with something to sell or, more often, with a poor animal that needed rescuing. We westerners were such saps for needy creatures.

Sure enough, the African Grey parrot they held out to me was needy. Its raw neck was surrounded by ragged feathers, pecked at in severe distress. The wing feathers had been brutally cropped to stop flight. The parrot's bottom was bare and bleeding, its brilliant red tail feathers plucked out and no doubt sold individually. Naturally enough it had anger on steroids and screeched horribly. I sighed and hardly allowed myself to utter the words, 'No. You go now. No come back. I buy nothing.' I was far too busy through the day and the caravan merely afforded me a bed and a bathroom, with absolutely no room for a pet. I closed the door.

Another knock on the door I ignored, and if they'd left it at that I would have too. But they knocked yet again, perhaps sensing my weakening resolve.

'No! I no buy,' But I did. So there we were, a furious parrot ready to take out all of its hate on me and me trying to manoeuvre around it. We had a mess room with a bar, where I ate fairly unimpressive meals and took my laundry. That's where I got some cashew nuts, their main diet I was reliably told, with all the will to make friends with the poor wretch. I put one down. Clearly hungry it slid its beak on the linoleum floor to get to it. Without tail feathers it couldn't balance to stand and could only move tripod fashion with beak and feet. 'Poor, sad, bugger!' I considered.

For now, though, my main objective was to get it in a better frame of mind, so that I could move around without being viciously attacked. I put my index finger forward, regretting a twitch in a nerve, and gingerly offered a nut to the ominous beak. Instantly the Grey's eyes fixed on the offending twitch, then on me, and back again. Filled with apprehension, I saw the beak open. And snap shut. Excruciatingly, with revenge enough to sever my finger. I expected to see blood. With equal reflexes I whisked free and swung back. A direct hit at its head sent it sliding and screeching across the slick floor and, bumph! Against the wall!

The bird returned. Sliding its beak toward me. This nutter wants more? Accustomed to being ill treated? With me another nutter, a foolish glutton for punishment, I again offered a nut on my finger. Except, expecting the same result, I wacked out first. Swoosh it went across the floor and bam! Into the wall!

The third time, was completely different. Its eyes fixed on me, its leathery grey tongue pushing purposefully at my finger, its beak opened almost caressingly to take the nut. Argue with me if you wish, but I saw understanding in that gaze. I was no enemy but a provider.

In South Africa recently, I occasioned upon an Indian woman in a convenience store who had an African Grey perched atop a cane of hers. She was by the door, hard to move past without getting close, and instinctively she cautioned me, 'Careful, he's vicious.' I was compelled to look, saw his anger, and reached my finger to him regardless. She was astonished, as the bird pushed at my finger with his tough grey tongue and did nothing more. I felt the same closeness as with my Grey, but always wondered how he felt anything toward me.

My travels on the Ughelli-Warri road took me past the glass factory that a German company had built and operated before the war. Everyone had been evacuated and now the buildings and bungalows for their expat staff lay abandoned yet in good condition. Tired of the long separation from Pam and Natasha I talked to Dave Gerber about it. To my amazement I was soon told that Shell-BP had acquired the compound for our use and I could bring my family out.

Aku was the name I was told when I acquired the parrot, I only knew later from Pam that this simply meant 'parrot' (not very inspired), and we two buddies moved to await Pam's arrival. We never changed Aku's name and never put him in a cage – fully knowing that he'd only learn to speak if we did that. He hopped about, with bright red feathers grown back, jumping onto sofas or the rim of

Natasha's pale blue paddling pool to be by our baby girl. Just like the family dog he'd waddle behind, through our machete groomed lawn, as we visited our neighbours. His wing feathers grew back and, on advisement, we had some discretely trimmed to prevent him flying away.

There were 12 bungalows and they soon filled with families, some with tales to tell of their transfer. Dave and Molly Sutton had a rough ride in. Their light aircraft ran out of fuel, or had a fuel blockage, near the river mouth at Forcados and had to ditch in the sea. Thankfully, though they'd seen no houses along the shoreline of trees, villagers had quickly despatched canoes to rescue passengers and their baggage.

Security was not great, just an unarmed guard in a hut at the wooden gate and no fencing to speak of. Some soldiers were occasionally stationed on the nearby roadside, which was a tad intimidating, and they made us laugh once. One of them had fired at a speck of an aircraft in the sky, with no way of knowing what it was and no chance of hitting it anyway.

Traders frequently walked in, straight out of the surrounding forests. From one, Pam rescued a bird, a black one, which she immediately released to our steward's astonishment.

I was at home when a barely clad trader walked out of the woods and sat before me on the terrace. Except this trader wasn't selling anything. Instead he gave me a story about a stash of ivory he had hidden in Biafra across the river – attempts to control and ban the trade began later, in the 1980s – which he wanted to retrieve. For that he needed funds. Looking back at all the experiences I'd had, at roadblocks and the bus collision especially, I now perceive something of the understanding that always took place. Yes, I was authoritative. Shell gave me that confidence, of someone the community looked up to. But that actually came from them. It always had done, back through the much-maligned British colonial era too. I wasn't asserting authority but rather it was expected of me. There's a huge difference between an authority enforced and one that's invited. Trustingly. You know the difference between working for someone you actually want authority from rather than one who forces it on you. The same goes between loving partners.

Somehow that trust meant something again now. I gave him the 500 Naira he wanted. Months later he was back on my terrace, thanking me for the loan and he repaid me in full. The mention of him paying interest fell on deaf ears and I wasn't concerned with that. A deal made had been honoured in full. And that was that. The man disappeared as he had first come, through the woods, and we never saw him again.

To help the wives with shopping trips to Warri, an 80 km round trip to the only village with the meagrest supply of western food, or actually not much of that at all, Shell-BP arranged for a minibus to take them there once weekly. Everything was

locally grown and barely nutritious or appetising –
eggs with whitish yokes, chicken tasting of the fish
they were fed on, beef from cattle walked off their
feet all the way (600 km) from the Obudu Cattle
Ranch on the border with Cameroon, milk only in
powdered form, vegetables with little lustre, and
just bananas, avocado pears, pawpaw, cashew nuts
and mangoes for variety. Spices were hard to find
and sauces non-existent. There was hardly any
choice in soft and alcoholic drinks, just the odd
bottle of cheap whisky, but with Coca Cola and Tiger
beer to spare everywhere.

The Shell-BP doctor's comment was that we
could get all the nutrients and protein needed from
just a diet of eggs and avocado pear.

The staple for locals comprised mainly of yam
and cassava, the latter chewed routinely gave them
among the healthiest and most beautifully white
teeth anywhere – though some, just a few, spoiled
that by going to teeth carvers, who shaped their
teeth into arrowheads or daggers. By comparison, in
the Far East, Asians with their non-dairy diet tended
to have teeth and complexions that were blotchily
unhealthy looking.

The retort we got when asking for fresh
vegetables at village restaurants, which Pam and I
would go to while other couples declined the
experience, was earnestly said with a mouthful of
good white teeth smiling, 'Yes masta. Fresh from de
tin.'

It was no exception at a really strange venue deep in a forest – Pam was itching to get out of the house, away from the niceties of visiting neighbours, and see something of the area – where, as it happened, we found our first steward. Built like a wooden stockade of pioneer days, complete with turrets on thick timber walls and a massive timber gate, it had bars full of laughing, fun Nigerians as well as 'professional ladies' and pounding live music.

Although we'd come alone as expats, and everywhere and everybody was black, we sensed no hostility whatever as we homed in to a basement restaurant. It was very dark and Pam was having difficulty with the hard contact lenses she then wore. She stumbled on the steps and the man, who would have a future in our lives, held her from falling flat on her face. Meal over, service good, we came right out with it, 'You dei wan work, for us?' We shook on it and Peter remained our faithful servant all the time we were in the Midwest state.

We were fortunate like that, with our stewards and cooks in each place. A commonly held view was that most robberies were an inside job and luckily, all credit to Pam, we never had a single theft in all of our eight years in Nigeria.

One day I had a weird feeling about the minibus taking the wives on their shopping trip. Completely unprompted by anything I followed far enough back not to be in anyway connected; at any other time there could have been light traffic, from our company vehicles as well as from local traders, but just then mine was the only other vehicle. My fears took shape on a straight section of road when the bus came to a stop. None were scheduled, never would be, before reaching Warri. Something was up. I let the distance shorten and then saw one of the wives alight. A soldier had stopped them, ordered her out, and now at gunpoint was walking her toward the treeline some 20 feet from the verge of the road. I eased the accelerator down, gradually getting closer and closer before the soldier saw a man in a car, my car. He stopped, I held back, and then he had to act. I veered gently to the edge of the road, in his direction, undeterred. Split seconds flashed by, the gap shrinking, his expression blank. And, then, slowly he motioned for her to return to the bus and turned out of sight.

The wife, whom I later learnt was Molly Sutton, got back aboard and the bus moved off. I stayed back to avoid any panic in the man, while letting the bus start off again, and managed to pass on the blind side out of his sights. Fortunately, that was the only incident with the minibus.

Another incident involved a soldier who stopped my car, Pam and Natasha with me, who wanted to trade at gunpoint. He pointed to our blond baby on the back seat, 'How much? I dei give you good price.' We smiled and slowly shook our heads, saying nothing, Pam as composed as I, and I simply drove on. He too had deferred to our authority, silently. We chuckled about it later, albeit nervously.

~*~

11   One of the Babies flew through

A pallid, featureless sky fused down into a wall of colourless grey trees surrounding our dull white bungalow, the tattered metalled roads we'd drive on and anywhere we'd go. The rainy season had started and it was pretty much like a curtain was blacking out sun, scenery and anything else. Except, there wasn't anything. Trees surrounding a building, road or clearing simply constituted the first line in an endless forest on the flat. There was no elevation, no vantage point, no way to see more. The frequent storms when thunder and lightning bellowed and flashed brilliantly, our corrugated roof clattered and roads ran like rivers, were hardly a welcome relief from the monotony.

'There's nowhere to see,' Pam whined plaintively, 'No views, anywhere.'

We were walled in, with no windows out of the sauna-like space. Sweat gleamed on our faces and our tops slapped onto our backs like cold towels as we entered into any air-conditioned homes, shops and offices. I remembered how, as a child, I'd smelt the sweet odour of sugar cane in the humid air of Barbados but here, where flowering plants were in little evidence, there was nothing of the sort.

The land was verdant though. It amazed me when walking down one of the surveyed lines, to check on clearing activities. The surveyors had cut branches to make pegs, which they'd painted yellow and driven into the ground to form the boundary. As my eye travelled along the parallel lines, I saw new shoots there. Growing on the painted pegs. The other thing that was shown to me by the contractor, was that some of the trees in the trace would fall over if leaned on. Farmers working this area had transplanted more trees, to add to their compensation. Every type of tree was listed with the price to be paid – and the trace was more thickly wooded than all around.

Shell-BP's standard accommodation had air conditioning in the bedrooms only, window units at that, with noisy compressors that took some getting used to; so there were sleep deprived nights and much of the time in the living areas we were in a sauna. On occasion, tears joined pearls of sweat as one of us complained of fatigue; the cure for dehydration, a tablespoon of salt in a glass of water.

Bugs were another problem, notably mosquitoes but also cockroaches in kitchen cabinets and weevils too in the rice. Another thing to watch out for was munching on bits of stone in the locally grown rice. Such was the rainy season that I'd whisked Pam and Natasha from a comfortable apartment in Walton-upon-Thames to share with me, in the event not without some grumbles.

It's incredible that Pam and the other wives didn't rant and rage more, considering they could not work. Work permit restrictions admirably enough favoured Nigerian over foreign skills – that's been the norm round the world but particularly there; the level of indigenisation in the work place went to 80% in the year I left. Actually, though, this was among measures that did not work for progress. The rush to democracy was too abrupt – a first step might well have included an *unelected* (appointed) Senate to steer tribal relations and the economy long-term, similar to the Hashemite Kingdom of *Jordan*'s House of Notables or the UK's House of Lords.

So, too, the rush to promise full indigenisation stirred emotions in elections but, in reality, it has driven the Nigerian oil industry, and the oil industry worldwide, into disrepute – Nigerian government estimates put oil spills since that time in the thousands and the volume at millions of barrels. Typically, this year (2015), Shell has agreed to pay a fishing community $83.5 million in compensation for oil spills.

A report on climate change (Pub: 2015. University College London) proposes deferring the exploitation of fossil fuels until carbon capture and storage techniques are perfected, estimated to be after 2050. If implemented, the impact on Nigeria's oil industry, and economy, would be disastrous and emphasises the need to grow and rebuild other industries as a matter of urgency.

Nigeria would be wise to pursue such policies in any event. Regardless, my view is that ways to raise standards and avoid deferring exploitation should be found instead – for oil in particular. Research that went into my science-based novel *DeepStorm OutTack* throws light on a far greater danger – that of an oil reservoir rupturing naturally in spurious seismic activity. The research supports speculation of an uncontrollable seepage of oil of that magnitude devastating the oceans and threatening life on Earth – as very likely it did 55 million years ago in the demise of dinosaurs.

In any case, Nigeria's indigenisation policies have been disastrous to other industries, with all sectors driven into decline or stagnation – though the most populated country in Africa (larger than Russia even) Nigeria's unemployment is now amongst the highest of major economies and poverty is also woefully high.

Such has been the haste for progress (and opportunity for greed and corruption) by ambitious political elites as well as by professional politicians. The opportunity missed, if the government would see it in the public interest long-term, is for Nigerian companies to instead pay for mentoring one-on-one to the highest international standards.

That means: twinning indigenous and foreign skills, both working together for say a couple of generations, with the aim of ultimate parity. Foreign companies involved in Nigeria's oil industry could kick this off; utilising funding offsets, such as from reduced claims, also better health and safety, but especially with targeting pollution-free standards acceptable to the staunchest of environmentalists (standards Shell-BP had when I was there).

Indigenisation restrictions are of little consequence, anyway, when the oil industry does not employ millions and other industries have fallen far behind the growth in population – The country's other industries have dropped to the point that petroleum products now account for 95% of exports. While the twinning approach would bring vitally needed skills to other sectors and revitalise the whole job market – with Nigeria's proximity to Europe it could easily compete with China there.

For the fullest effect, I envisage the approach being extended to the public sector and even government. The greatest impediment to Nigerians is not their incapability but in the country's lack of organisational infrastructure – even the physical infrastructure is in disrepair. It's the same throughout Africa. As an example of attracting high-level skills note that one of the most important public posts in the UK today, Governor of the Bank of England, is held by Canadian Mark Carney.

Anyway enough said on politics, I'll return to our personal lives there. Getting out and about meant dicing with oncoming traffic for the little amount of road between potholed verges; and, in downpours, holes large enough for a person or car to plunge into could be concealed.

George Parker, the British manager of Mothercat, was in the back seat of his Mercedes when he fell asleep on the long journey to Lagos. The added obstacles in dicing with oncoming traffic on that journey were the bridges, with just one lane, that dotted the route at rivers. George found himself, Mercedes and all, immersed in water when his driver chickened out at the last moment when going headlong towards a truck. The instant the truck filled the bridge George's driver aborted and drove off the road, down the bank. He went straight into the river. George woke to find water all around him. Needless to say, wrecked and rusting vehicles were a common feature around those bridges.

There still the pressure of completing pipelines, and it didn't help at all that I'd now been infected with a filarial parasite. My left arm became so swollen and heavy, though not painful, that it was useless for changing gear when driving (vehicles drove on the left then). The doctor put me on a dose of banocide. He didn't hold out much hope of getting rid of the parasite, which had entered my system as larvae on the stinger of a mosquito. He said there'd be a male and female worm laying eggs in my blood, the banocide hopefully keeping them from hatching. My best hope, was for one of the parents to be seen crawling across my eyeball. The doctor could then attempt to pluck it out. Otherwise they'd live in me forever.

That was not the prognosis I wanted. When nothing seemed to be happening I doubled the dose, and over the next few weeks kept doubling it. I think I reached 16 or 32 tablets a day. Nothing seemed to work, my heavy arm always a burden in the car even when stopped at a roadblock. The drill was always the same, a soldier demanding, 'Open de boot'. I wound the window back up and went round to open the boot. Fatigued by the arm I left them to look for whatever and to close it again. 'Fine', I was waved on.

One day at a second roadblock, 'Open de boot'. I went round, opened it and stood back startled. The soldier was gaping at an automatic rifle lying there on the floor. The soldier at the previous roadblock had put it down to search with both hands and forgotten it. Now I don't know if they'd had any communication, it's hardly likely as theirs wasn't great, or if this was not that unusual an event, or what, but they didn't get all excited and arrest me. 'You go,' they waved me on.

Finally I had an itch on my arm. On scratching it a fine transparent thread, no bigger than a hair, came out. I hadn't dared hope that this was a parent but gradually the swelling eased and disappeared. The filarial parasite was done for, or one of the parents was; and, as far as I was concerned, the other in me could just die of loneliness.

My work was just about complete and with great relief we prepared to go on a generous holiday. Before leaving we asked a neighbouring family, the Van De Hoeckes, who loved animals and had several of their own, to look after Aku. He could stay in a cage whenever needed and his diet of cashew nuts was simple enough. Or that's what we thought. We were devastated, Pam and Natasha as much as myself, to learn on our return that he'd refused to eat and seemingly pined away. African Greys can get terribly attached to their owners and we suspected his trauma was about his rescuer and caring new family having abandoned him.

Shortly after, the military situation took a new turn when Count von Rosen took sides to help the Biafrans – Count Carl Gustaf Ericsson von Rosen, a Swede, was turned down by the RAF in World War II because, by happenstance, he became a nephew-in-law of Gestapo founder Herman Goering. He'd flown relief missions in other countries and arrived at the Biafran military base, Uli, flying a DC7 at wave height from the nearby island of São Tomé. The Biafran cause attracted others and he formed the Biafran Babies, comprising five civilians (including three Biafrans) with single engine SAAB trainers fitted out only with unguided grenade launchers. They flew well below radar at tree top level and swooping low over Nigerian Air Force airfields they managed to destroy several Soviet supplied and operated MIG-17 fighters and three Ilyushin bombers (half of the fleet). Von Rosen left shortly after destroying the Ughelli power station while the Babies went on to hit airfields and other facilities right up to the end of the war. The federals did succeed in following two of the Babies, the MIG strafing the SAABs once parked on the ground.

Whether or not it was the count, as was reported in the papers, or another of the Babies, but one of Shell-BP's drilling rigs was targeted, injuring expat drillers. I hadn't considered it before, but now see that this was not random. Rather, it was a tactic

74

aimed at delaying oil revenues from funding the federal military campaign. Widely reported is the assumption that this had already begun. More likely is that the Soviet Union and Czechoslovakia provided credit for their military support, the largest in the federal campaign. Possibly likewise when Britain's Prime Minister Harold Wilson acted, against the will of the people and of parliament, in exceptionally providing the federals with 36 Saladin and Saracen armoured cars accompanied by machine guns, ammunitions and two helicopters.

A grenade went through the ventilation ducts of the glass factory next to our houses and exploded in the Sutton's garden. Adding to tensions, a Biafran raiding party crossed the Niger and took 11 drillers hostage from an Elf drilling platform just half an hour's drive away from us. Weeks went by before the French government negotiated their release, even though with Charles de Gaulle as President France supported the Biafrans.

It was about this time that the heads of Nigeria and breakaway Biafra, respectively Yakubu Gowon and Odumegwu Ojukwu, met in Addis Ababa, Ethiopia; where they failed to reach any compromise and bring the war to a peaceful conclusion. The meeting did, however, put the spotlight on Biafra. Horrifying photos of starving children began to emerge; several mercenaries were flying for the Biafran Air Force and they might have brought some out. With mounting international pressure, foreign reporters were granted limited access and The International Committee of the Red Cross among others fought for a corridor through which to airlift humanitarian aid. That was as much as anyone knew at the time, with no hint of the atrocities that were yet to be uncovered.

It was clear, though, that the situation had turned considerably uglier than previously imagined and Shell-BP moved our families to the safety of the camp in Warri. Not long after, the day came to commission the Ughelli Quality Control Centre, with pipelines that we'd worked on for streaming oil via the Forcados Terminal. One of the Babies flew through, possibly Count Von Rosen, as the papers again reported, and put grenades at several heights in the main tank. To no avail, Shell-BP had delayed the commissioning, possibly on a hunch, but possibly too with good intelligence. The same insightful management had given us, me certainly, confidence in our safety.

Personally, I had no sense of it then and see no evidence of it now that Shell-BP, or its principals, had prevailed on western governments to interfere militarily. That's what many people have been led to believe and thus have protested ceaselessly against oil companies across the globe that they're eager to preserve lucrative interests by waging war for oil. Yet, we had no military escorts or guards at the offices or oil facilities – not that we'd have welcomed them. No troops came from Britain in a concerted rescue action – crossing the Niger River to Stan Grey under house arrest in Onitsha and steaming up the Bonny River to us in Port Harcourt; which would have been easy for Britain's crack SAS corps. The Biafrans weren't well armed, they had no funds for that. Nor were we held at gunpoint, as the hostages of terrorists are – the Biafrans weren't terrorists. Rather, we were 'guests' (reminiscent of Patrick McGoohan in the British TV series *The Prisoner*) free to move around but not leave the rebel territory. Hostage or captive situations vary and, in reality, ours had become a more open style of house arrest than the expatriate captives of Iraqis were subjected to in the Gulf War (which was another nightmare that eventually awaited Pam).

The reason for all of this, I believe, is that in its best interests Shell-BP had to deal directly with both warring parties. The federal and Biafran governments both lay claim to Shell-BP's limited licences to explore and produce oil. In the end, with no sign that the war would soon be over, and the ploy of maintaining the payment of oil revenues had played out (production had ceased), Shell-BP simply had to pay – as said, £1 million was paid in cash for Stan Grey's release and with that our own freedom.

Commerce is tough, in a world of tough players, as was the case of the British West Africa administration's bias towards British trading interests with Nigeria. For Shell-BP it was again business in a tough place at a tough time, but now it had to get on and produce oil regardless of the government of the day.

What has to be levelled about the Biafran War is that Ojukwu and Adekunle were both abhorrent of the power play of their political elites that cost over a million lives and held back the economy and welfare of many more millions – a sentiment about political elites that can be extrapolated globally, to the present day, and involving tens if not hundreds of millions.

Port Harcourt

12   I have to kill the Ibos

With facilities for starting production completed in the Midwest state, our next move was to Lagos where we were provided with an apartment on the upmarket suburb island of Ikoyi. It was nice, with two bedrooms and near to the Lagos Motor Boat Club, Ikoyi, to which we had membership.

Before settling in, though, we took a long-earned holiday – three months to relax and de-stress in – and, as one does at that age, Pam and I set off house hunting in the UK. We found a beautiful thatched, lath and stud house in St. Neots but, difficult as it was to afford getting on the housing ladder – in my 20s I was not on a huge salary – so, we ended up buying a flint farmhouse in North Wales and hiring an architect to convert the adjoining barn. We found an inglenook fireplace and made a balconied living room out of the barn. As this was to be our home we were well received by our neighbours. We lived there as work began and, blessed with beautiful weather, had Natasha's paddling pool by the front door step to bath in. At last, we had a home of our own!

Alas, on returning to Lagos, we found that I was only going to be there four days a fortnight. My assignment was to build pipelines in the swamps to the west of Bonny Terminal and Port Harcourt, occupying 1,900 square kilometres this has the largest area of mangrove in Africa.

The imponderables we faced, with the neglect war had inflicted on the region, were flagged up on the first trip in from Lagos. This was a no-fly zone and after several weary hours, across over 650 km at sea on a passenger vessel named 'Chikensaw' (which we dubbed 'Chickenshit', it was such a rough ride), we ran aground on a sandbank up the Bonny River, en route to Port Harcourt.

Bonny and the Bonny River had just recently been recaptured by the 3rd Marine Commandos, a naval action launched from Calabar with support from the Nigerian Navy frigate Nigeria and boats *expropriated* from Shell-BP. The commander was the mythically ruthless Colonel Benjamin Adekunle; who previously, before our living there, had retaken Ughelli and Warri from the Biafrans.

Adekunle, quoted in Stern Magazine (Germany), on the blockade of aid to Biafra: 'on the whole south front from Lagos to the border of Kamerun [Cameroon] I do not want to see the Red Cross, Caritas Aid, World Church delegation, Pope, Missionary, or UN delegation... I did not want this war but I want to win this war. Therefore, I have to kill the Ibos. Sorry! The End.'

The plan of the Head of State, General Gowon, was genocide. The "Black Scorpion", as Adekunle became known, went on to use reprisals, bombing villages, schools and hospitals, to prompt Biafran soldiers into disengaging from hostilities. 'Shock and awe' was his declared aim and, with that tactic, he has been accredited – legendarily – with having turned the tide of the civil war.

A world figure now, a showman in the eyes of all, including the international press, the Black Scorpion had struck at the underbelly of Biafra with his 3rd Marine Commandos' assault on Port Harcourt; when, surprisingly, he is reported to have ordered the same tactic of 'shock and awe' in approaching not a military target but the village of Peterside. The loudest cannon fire boomed over the one-storey houses, sending everyone scurrying. Then, unimaginably, one battle-hardened figure, the massacring Black Scorpion, walked the empty streets and knocked on the door of a private compound.

He knocked, knocked and knocked. Receiving no answer, he later recalled fearing that, rather than forcing inhabitants to seek shelter, he'd scared them all into the bush. In a final attempt, he shouted through the door, 'Comfort... Akiye, it is me Papa Sola'. A soft wailing cry was heard before his young Igbo wife opened the door and tumbled into his arms. She had visited parents when the war broke out and remained there since.

Quirkily, in this brutal war, having vowed to kill the *Igbos* this small man of mixed ethnicity (his father was from the Yoruba west while his mother from a Bachama district in the north), had rescued none other than his *Igbo* spouse.

Adekunle took up residence in the MD's office of Shell-BP's former head quarters *expropriated* by the

Commandos. My bosses made do in Shell-BP's operational offices.

Meanwhile my quarters were in a houseboat, with generator barge and mess barge, which we anchored as well as we could in the swamp close to Bonny. Ominously, Bonny was remembered as the 'white man's grave'; where tombstones in a cemetery are of young men, sons that did not inherit their father's large estates and instead tried their hand in the colonies. Life expectancy, notably with Malaria a constant threat, was reputed to be just six months.

We had dangers other than disease – being fairly well protected by taking (antimalarial) paludrine tablets – in that the weight of our barges tied together, in strong currents and changing tides, pulled perilously on lines to muddy river bottom anchors and lines to small mangrove trees. Gauging the force of the current, by eye, I wasn't happy with our first anchorage. That night with all of us asleep, I was woken to see trees moving past us. We were moving downstream, the whole line of barges was, to where the creek met the vast and deep Bonny River – there at its mouth, it was as wide as the Mississippi. Once into its grip, where the anchors would be useless, we'd be swept over the nearby sand bar and capsized in the waves breaking at sea. We still had lights, with the generator barge still connected to the houseboat, and I called on the radio for tugs to get there, urgently. Hours later, the manoeuvre accomplished, we'd survived the harrowing night.

After that event we became pretty expert at resetting anchors, as the work moved further and further along the long route. By contrast the poorly maintained outboard engines of our dinghies, which all too often left us stranded, were a bane we never got used to. Yet, for all that, my task of keeping all intact and the team of inspectors effective – who, it has to be said, were a surly bunch – was a small part of chasing progress with the work, on a war front.

My tours of duty were tough on Pam, having to manage alone, raise toddler Natasha, and still without the freedom to work. Well enough read in literature and the arts, far more so than engineer me, and with sound experience as a secretary, it frustrated her no end to be stuck at home. She'd have been far happier doing something productive, such as mentoring a local secretary or PA to the benefit of everyone all round. It's a shame, a great waste, for government policy to have prohibited work permits for such foreigners instead of encouraging one-on-one mentoring.

There was no particular problem with her driving around Ikoyi – by comparison, today, British Airways apparently expects crew to stay within the grounds of their hotel and only travel between there and the airport under armed guard. Nevertheless, the isolation Pam felt led to at least one outburst involving dinner plates being broken at my feet. Her red hair belied a fiery Irish strain from her mother but she was more deflated than angry at that moment; and I felt for her, without being able to do anything about it. All we could do was to put my progression in Shell foremost and stick it out. I too missed out, on family life and on those early days of Natasha growing up. Such was the commitment we'd made, with the pressure of building pipelines again taking my full attention.

Except, now the stakes were much higher. Top international contractors were engaged, mobilising some of the most powerful and costly equipment used anywhere in terrestrial pipeline construction. Over 100 km of large bore pipe was to be laid and buried, every inch of it through swamp and under more than 60 rivers and creeks – several of which were large, with the largest crossing right at the mouth of the Bonny River.

Clearing crews started on several fronts and dredgers began digging ditches. But, there was soon a problem. The main lay barge was ready, a flat top barge long enough to appear like a small aircraft carrier; except, it's long line of pipe racks and welding stations stood empty. There was no pipe. The barge was to creep forward, lowering the welded and coated line off the stern, except now it would stay idle and clock up costly claims for demurrage.

The main contractor, Santa-Fe Pomeroy, called me to a meeting that forever changed my viewpoint on American ingenuity. The first shipment of pipe was aboard a purpose-built vessel, fitted with the drop-down bow of a landing craft. However, surveys of the bar across the mouth of Bonny River revealed that the ship could not pass over it fully laden. They'd dredged out a new harbour, at the seashore end of Bonny, but it proved impossible to achieve the depth needed for the ship's draft. The harbour entrance was through the beach and kept filling with sand. Powerful Manitowoc cranes were at work but, even at 4,000 hp apiece, they couldn't dig the sand out quickly enough. Nor was there enough muscle to drag the vessel in. The problem seemed insoluble, a brick wall.

Ah, but Texans don't see brick walls. They love a challenge. They'd done their sums with the shipping company, and the answer was as audacious as it was simple. 'The reason we asked you to this meeting,' they said, 'is to put this to you. We can't pull the ship into the harbour. But, we calculate that there's enough muscle to pull *half* of it in.' If they expected the solution to dawn on me then, and their gazes suggested that, they were disappointed. 'We want to cut the vessel in half. Mid-ship, between the bulkheads.'

You'll have noticed by now, how on occasions I was faced with an inability to contribute to a discourse. When I met the NEPA manager in Warri, for instance. This now was such an event. Except I did ask, 'Do the ship's owners agree with this?'

'We've spoken with them, discussed terms, and they have no objection.'

I had to think fast. 'The contract with Shell-BP is turnkey, so there's no cost implication to them.' There were nods of agreement all round. 'And "time is of the essence",' That too was met with nods. 'So, Shell-BP can have no objection. It's your undertaking, your cost. Your call.'

It was amazing. They went ahead, and cut the hull, for the Manitowocs to then drag half the ship to where they could offload the pipes. The other half was dealt with the same way. Then well, of course(!), they welded the vessel together again for the return journey. The whole procedure went as smoothly as a NASA engineered project.

The main lay barge, smaller lay barges at river crossings, Manitowocs cutting ditches, dredgers in rivers and tugboat captains working the currents to keep barges on line, were all soon active in an area of several hundred square kilometres.

The scene was incredible: the swamp a mirror of the sky in all its moods as big as the horizons at high tide, a peat billiard table bristling with sharp mangrove shoots and scored by tree lined creeks and rivers at low tide. All was cased in a desert-like silence, away from the clamour of pipe welding, with the pulse and rhythm of water like none other on Earth. The spirits of this serenity were egrets – white ones foretelling the approach of the dry season and black the wet season, and two together when there was a snake close by – as well as spiders, small birds, mud-skippers and crabs. I once saw a web with yellow strands looking like twisted cord, big enough to catch a small bird, and didn't wait to see the spider. I rarely saw monkeys and never a crocodile, not even the West African dwarf croc native to the delta – I wondered if the tidal waters were too brackish.

Taking a break from engineering, as well as the drudgery of houseboat maintenance or human relations or outboard engines failing, I occasionally fished. I did that especially during the protracted operation of laying pipe across the Bonny River. Several large tugboats were needed to keep the cutter-suction dredger on course in the fast flowing channel, for digging the ditch straight, and then the barge pulling the welded pipe from the far bank. A large houseboat office was anchored there, for Santa-Fe Pomeroy engineers to be in full attendance.

I could only watch, so I fished in glorious sunshine. The magic came with recognising the way the waters flowed off the flat peat, sweeping small fish and crustaceans into creeks and then to large rivers. It was at the mouth of a creek, in full view of the main activity, that the delicious *shiny nose* waited and where I trawled my favourite lure.

I landed a beaut, weighing 30lb, which went in the camp freezer and filled a suitcase for me to take home. Another time I took a visiting Shell-BP engineer, Alan Hunt, trawling. He exclaimed after the line went taut and finally broke, 'If that thing was getting in here,' he'd seen how big the shiny nose was, compared with the size of our boat, 'I was getting out!' To my dismay that was my favourite lure and no other worked for me as that did.

Conscientious about progress I was into all activities and on occasions even joined the surveyor, John Redfern, in walking the ditch waste deep through swamp. We never came across anything dangerous in the murky water but, in our concentration, walked face first into spider webs. At times I donned scuba gear at a river crossing, feeling with my hands to check the concrete coating of pipe sunk there. Visibility was zero, save for the fluorescent sparkle of plankton.

As that illustrated this vast and beautiful no-man's-land was worth gazing at. I watched a heavily set woman approach the shallows from a riverbank. Wading in, she lifted her skirt-length wrap higher and higher as she slowly went deeper and deeper. To my surprise she was moving with difficulty deep in mud and then plopped down to sit on it. Somehow that scene of a woman tending a fish trap, habitually surrounded by free flowing water, had me thinking about the aquatic ape theory and the evolution of humans that I'd read something on.

Raymond Rice, an exceptionally tall and well-built Texan, was the spread boss on the main lay barge. One day, crooking my neck to eye him, I dutifully advised, as I'd been instructed by my American boss Walter Nanny, that the Minister of Mines and Power was visiting. He was coming down from Lagos and would alight on Rice's deck from a helicopter. Rice scanned his domain, mulled something over, and then made his position clear. He had no issue with *whatever* the Minister wanted to see, 'Except. He does *not* go in there.' He pointed to the mess room. 'He can go wherever he God damned likes. *But* not there!'

My nerves tightened in knowing, absolutely, that nothing about the visit was negotiable. My bosses would not accept any climb down, not where the Ministry of Mines and Power was concerned. 'He owns this whole project,' I twisted my neck to see a reaction. 'He can shut us down in a flash.' It was an awkward stance to try being assertive from down there, looking up, and all I could do was rely on a calm, firm tone getting through.

'Well. If that nigger goes in there,' he quizzed me with a stern look, 'I won't be responsible for the consequences.'

The expat crew were a rough and tough mix of redneck Texans and Creoles. One, a cheerful tugboat captain named Jay Tipedo, returned from a trip home in New Orleans with a gunshot wound in his foot. He laughed as he told me, 'Got in an argument, in a bar. The guy went home. Came back with a pistol!' Some were not unlike a smart Texan manager I worked under, over a decade later with another employer; he came back from a home visit boasting about a 'Klan' event he'd taken part in, when they caught a black man and played at hanging him.

I greeted the arrivals, most particularly the Minister, and quickly introduced Raymond who led the way in guiding them round. The body language was neither strained nor stressed, with all concerned showing interest and appreciation for what was being accomplished. Raymond eyed me as they approached the mess room – where nothing at all happened.

The prime objective for cooperation between Shell-BP and the Ministry, was building oil revenues; which fitted the company's profit incentive. Conflicting with this, and the need to curtail risks of oil spillage, was continuing social unrest centred around local empowerment (creating jobs); Shell-BP's resources, as with other Western companies, were too thin on the ground to safely escalate their transformation of technical skills at that time, throughout the war. As I've indicated elsewhere, the focus should instead have been on using oil revenues to transform skills in other industries.

Regardless, and largely also because the Western companies had not supported the war effort (rather, one French oil company had supported Biafra) in the year after the war finally ended, the Nigerian Government established the Nigerian National Oil Corporation (NNOC) and acquired stakes in Shell-BP and other Western companies operating in the oil industry.

Possibly, there is the opportunity to bring the oil industry and empowerment back on track – now. Muhammadu Buhari was democratically elected President of Nigeria in May 2015 and it is speculated that he will keep the petroleum minister portfolio for himself in the new cabinet. He is well acquainted with the issues. In the mid 1970s Major General Buhari took office as Federal Commissioner for Petroleum Resources and first Chairman of NNPC (Nigerian National Petroleum Corp).

Of course, in my engineering capacity, I knew nothing of such developments at the time.

The lay barges moved inexorably through the swamp's river system, diggers crawling and clanging like *War of the Worlds* Martian machines from one river to the next over the peat. Unlike pipe laying on land, where the pipe grows length by length and goes straight into ditches, the pipe out there seemed to extrude sausage-machine-like from barges and push along floating in ditches – one river to the next.

I'd pick solitary vantage points to listen to the incredible silence and the faint sound of Martians in the distance – a view I never tired of and found so refreshing after the viewless Midwest – and watched the coated pipe lying snake-like in the vast peat's sky-reflecting waters. I could only wonder at the thoughts of fishermen paddling along small creeks as they occasioned upon this barrier from hell. There was no going round it, long as it was. At least, self-reliant and remote as they were from the Biafran heartland, they'd been spared from bombings and starvation, as far as I could tell.

On one such occasion I watched two bemused fishermen, crouched in their canoe. They'd stopped at the pipe and seemed to ponder in dismay about some destination beyond it. I'd cruised round to join an English inspector of ours, landing my boat next to his, to learn that he'd just spoken with them. Thankfully relations were convivial as ever, despite the war, but he was smirking, 'I just told them. We have magic!'

'Oh,' was all I could reply. We both looked at the men and further along the pipe for as long as we could see it. We then turned to look in the other direction, to where the pipe disappeared round a clump of trees. There was a longish wait, during which I kept in radio contact with a lay barge out there, and we cast the occasional glance at the men. Finally the moment arrived, when the snake, where it came round the trees, sank below the surface and continued to sink towards us, then past us and past the astonished looks of the fishermen and beyond. Of the solid pipe of steel that couldn't be budged suddenly, without the slightest sound, all trace of it had gone. They looked our way expressionless and, yet, somehow all-knowing, as if expecting magic from us. Of course, they couldn't know about a barge that, on schedule, pumped water behind a 'pig' (a rubber cup) to fill and sink the pipe.

Thankfully, despite the proximity of the Biafran front line, we saw no military activity, although we had an incident with one of my clearing inspectors who went missing, miles ahead of the main activity. Three days later his bloated body came to the surface and it was clear he'd been killed.

I wasn't there, having gone on holiday. In England we made a beeline to see Pam's mum and gran and then straight to our home in North Wales. This time it was in winter and deep snow was briefly on the ground. By contrast we next flew to the warmth of the Seychelles to visit my parents George and Sylvia on Mahe. He was Director of Tourism and my mother had been helping with arrangements for Queen Elizabeth II's visit to open the new airport.

On my return to Nigeria Ted Jackson, who'd stood in for me, told me that the army had received word of a village where a suspect was hiding. He'd gone to the troops on their houseboat, which we'd not realised was anchored round a bend in the river, to see if they would board his launch to go up river. To his amazement the sergeant counted out a handful of bullets each, only to discover that they'd not enough to go around. He took them all back, returning them to the carton, and handed out fewer bullets this time. It took three goes. Hastening them along it was only after they'd sped up the river some distance, he up front next to the skipper, that Ted wondered about the sanity of being there. Was it sane? Him being there. As it happened, the suspect had fled the village.

We'd seen some news of the war. The humanitarian corridor into Biafra had focused on areas around the Uli airstrip, a section of road converted for the purpose, with reporters able to cover those environs. But around this time the airlift was closed by the federals.

Supplies had come in by sea but with considerable waste, deliberate or otherwise. On my visits to Port Harcourt the pall of smoke pouring out from the docks was unmistakable. Shiploads of powdered milk were added to a mountain that burnt for the whole year I was there. Sent there by well-meaning aid agencies, it was burnt by the federals – on the grounds that Igbo babies weren't able to digest it.

I learnt from others that they'd seen ambulances with Red Cross markings being unloaded from vessels at Apapa Docks, Lagos, and soon after those same vehicles had federal army markings.

I've long been appalled at the humanitarian aid that failed to reach Biafra; and, rather naively as it happens, I'd imagined funds as well as provisions that were siphoned off by fat cat executives or administrators, as well as by corrupt government officials and agents.

It's clear to me now how the federals had not only frustrated foreign reporting but also disrupted aid supplies – there are reports of shipments attacked mid-air and bombed on the ground in refugee camps and in hospitals by the federal air force. At the end of the second year a flight of the International Committee of the Red Cross was shot down by a Nigerian Air Force MIG. The Red Cross was then deported; and the airlifts were restricted to daylight operations and federal inspections.

Frustrated by all of this, and by the resulting impotence of the Red Cross, the year after the end of war ten French physicians led by Bernard Kouchner (later to become French foreign minister) created a team that would become known as "Doctors Without Borders" (Médecins Sans Frontières) expressly to help the people in the Nigerian region of Biafra.

~*~

13   You bring the girl who is not there

After the war was over I was assigned a bungalow in the refurbished Umukoroshe. The eeriest thing happened on my first day when breakfasting, at the camp restaurant, at a table that happened to face the bungalow I'd lived in many months previously. Lying on the carport roof were two cats, one ginger and one black and white – the exact same markings as the cats the doctor had to put down. They were looking straight at me. That was the only sighting. I never saw either, ever again.

Those two aside, everything looked rosier than in all the months that had gone before for us, in Nigeria, with the sun shining through the wall-to-wall windows and prospects for a normal life awaiting. The camp looked so inviting with its newly painted walls, cut lawns, trimmed trees and blossoming flowerbeds. I couldn't wait to bring Pam and Natasha 'home' there.

Meanwhile, I moved into the new bungalow and began to get it ready. Naturally, I socialised a bit too with the guys at work. We had some good laughs – such as seeing one wife frantically undressing on the golf green. Oblivious of the gaze of us at the clubhouse, she pulled down her trousers and even her panties. To get at an ant biting her crotch!

With the new pipelines in the swamp all tested and ready for operation, I was available to assist with troubleshooting. The task of re-commissioning the old facilities would take months but enough of the largest ones had been prioritised to get production started. Almost immediately there was an oil leak reported in Cawthorne Channel, a large river in the swamp. I got there quickly by helicopter and by radio got confirmation from Production that they'd reduced the flow in the pipe. The contractor had already mobilised men and equipment and their site manager was surveying the black oil shining on the surface of the water. There was no need for him to appraise me of the situation, as I got that directly from the two expat divers who just then came out of the water.

They'd found the pipe in the river bottom but after several attempts failed to locate the leak. The current was strong, the visibility zero and they'd little idea of what to look for. I described the concrete coating on the pipe and that they should look for a break in that, but gained no confidence in what they were taking in. I didn't have that much confidence in what to look for myself and time was short. Decision time, I asked to join them in another dive.

To my relief they kitted me out with a state-of-the-art dry suit, which had a helmet with built in intercom. We waded in with me in the lead, feeling for the pipe. Going forward, deeper and deeper, I was soon immersed in darkness with plankton sparkling all around me. I'd encountered that before in these swamps, except now I could feel barnacles on the concrete and soon enough there was the heat of the oil. The visibility really went to zero. To my relief my fingertips groped at steel mesh, which had reinforced the now broken away concrete. That was it, the gash in the pipe was there – doubtless caused by an anchor in naval operations.

Shortly after Pam and Natasha arrived, I was assigned an office as Administration Engineer to Chief Engineer Wilhelm Veltman. He and his wife, Jos, a very social couple, welcomed the wives coming in with a party at their home. They carried on the Shell tradition of mixing outside of work, emphasising to do that one rank up and one rank down. I reckon that had more to do with connecting on the work front, than anything to do with class or snobbery.

The community grew from that point on, with Pam and I welcoming Chris and Dian Fenner on their arrival. We introduced them to playing bridge and were astonished to hear that they'd become hooked on it – often playing to the small hours of the morning. They left Shell sometime later and emigrated to America, he having authored a book on management. Among other Shell friends were Chris and Jenny Fay.

We also befriended some families of expat service companies, living away from Umukoroshe, and one such had a narrow escape. Marching ants had gone right past their house one night and even forced the local police station to be evacuated. They left a trail of devastation, which included their garden birdcage. Incredibly, they found not only skeletons of their birds but also a snake with a bird in it.

Not being one to sit about or join in coffee mornings as usual Pam wanted to see the countryside, so we ventured to outlying villages and once even took our car on a locally made raft that served as a ferry. Strikingly, villagers away from the town had neither electricity nor piped water and, yet, they would be seen sweeping the ground around their huts and collectively having the pride to keep their community clean. We'd seen the same disparity between town and rural lifestyles in the Midwest; and I saw the same more recently in South Africa. By comparison, in China there is neglect just about anywhere in the countryside and even in areas of natural beauty. I believe that says something of the pride and sense of community that prevailed in rural Nigeria; something that some of Britain could learn from, let alone other parts of the world.

What we saw no signs of around Port Harcourt, were the reported ravages or starving in this war. Somehow, as in the Midwest where we knew there'd been mass killings, none of that was in open view to our untrained eyes.

We had very few experiences of the sort, this time in PH. My office door opened one day to a chief of no noteworthy build or dress, who wanted to discuss payment for work done on roads. As courteous as we all were, I referred him to the Civil Engineer for his area, who was just down the corridor. 'No,' he said, 'You see, dis engineer not be from my tribe.'

The engineer in question was also Nigerian. The chief rather wanted to discuss things with an engineer who was impartial, which meant dealing with me as a white man. He even said that was the case under British administration, and wished that could return. I did not sway and he did go to the engineer in question. It worked, the chief never came back. That was because, basically, regardless of the individual engineer, Shell-BP's dominantly European culture was simply meritocratic – ethnicity had no place, and never could in any of its places of business.

Nigeria's indigenisation policies have long since put an end to all of that. Along with spin about bad colonials – some references to injustices have been warranted but not, in this context, on the scale publicised – all of that has been devastatingly counter productive in isolating Nigerian workforces from white Europeans. The bad press has masked how the estrangement has impoverished Nigeria's industries, and robbed them from becoming part of the incredible transformation that has taken place in the European Union. For the benefit of just a few elites, who enjoy being free of meaningful governance, in its isolation Nigeria (and most of Africa) has digressed to poverty on the streets while the EU has gone on to become a major powerhouse of the modern world – and a huge magnet to the latest 'out of Africa' migration, across the Mediterranean and up through Arabia.

Part of the attraction is Europe's standing as a caring society. Veltman was also the Dutch Vice Consul for the region and he received word that a Dutch girl was being held against her wishes in one of the villages. As with most villages, this one had a contract for road works and Veltman summoned the chief to our offices. With me present, he came straight out with it, 'I'm told that there's a white girl in your village.' He went on to enquire about her well-being.

'No! Dere be no white dere.'

Further probing solicited the same result, leaving my boss with no alternative. A big man very capable of bellowing, he nonetheless remained civil as usual, 'OK. You have contracts with us?' He only paused long enough for the chief to nod. 'Your contracts are all cancelled. Unless, tomorrow morning, you bring the girl who is not there to my office, together with her passport.'

The girl arrived with the chief. She'd met and married her husband in Delft University, Holland, and travelled with him to his home near Port Harcourt. The fun and laughter that had attracted her vanished as she was expected to attend to the home, a hut in the village. By the time of her discovery, she had been stripped of money and passport and was tethered to the hut. Now she was again free. What Veltman lamented, as we all did, were all the other white girls out there that would never be discovered or helped – let alone countless girls of other ethnicities.

It is not only girls who need such caring. The company only provided quarters for a steward and a cook, which was not unusual there. Later, when we got to Lagos, it was different in that there were family quarters for them. On a personally sad note, our steward in Umukoroshe was coughing blood and, diagnosed with turberculosis, had to leave the camp. The company would not run the risk of contaminating others. Shell-BP's doctor gave him a supply of tablets and Pam and I, having no choice in the matter, gave him six months salary. What grieved us was hearing from neighbours that this was futile. 'When he gets to his village, they will take that from him.'

~*~

Lagos

14 I read Ojukwu's book...He was right

I was next relocated to Shell-BP's head offices in Lagos. I'd had yet another long stretch working and with six weeks to holiday I'd booked an Alitalia flight to Rome, which included a mobile home in which to tour Italy. The first of its kind there, the unit was brand new and with all campsites already closed, it was autumn, we just roamed wherever we pleased – viewing old towns and ancient ruins, of course wine and food too, from Rome to Paestum, Metaponto, Assisi, Gubbio, Urbino, Verona, Vicenza, Padua. Venice, Florence, Siena. Natasha, a happy blue eyed blond of three, got so much attention everywhere that she was passed from table to table in some trattorias.

We got so lost with all the one-way roads getting into Citta Vecchia in Urbino that we ended up looking at a flight of stairs. Yeah, with nothing more for it, I drove the mobile home bumpity bump up the steps. This was nothing compared with everything we'd been through. A woman with a basket of laundry at the top shrieked and ran, dropping everything. A policeman mouthed, 'Stranieri!', shook his head and moved off.

My new job in Nigeria was as Senior Engineer Production Facilities responsible for designing oilfield plant. That was possibly the most challenging and fun assignment of my long working life. Designs started with various assumptions to do with the fields that were to be brought on line. We had the wet season to pin down everything for the design and sizing of equipment: the grade of oil, the gas and water ratio, the pressure. Most vital were their locations. The trouble was, the wells that would confirm any of that had yet to be drilled.

Murals resembling Banksy's art, or perhaps the major incident room of a crime investigation, filled one room. There hung the results of seismic surveys and graphics of whatever could be gleaned about rock structures deep under ground that geologists and petroleum engineers worked on studiously.

My interest was in the equally artistic drilling schedule, with rows for the many drilling rigs (eleven I seem to remember) and strips of coloured paper for the type of drilling and pins flagging the locations. Unlike other murals these were constantly changing, as seismic and drilling results poured in, and I had to constantly adjust plans to suit.

The trick was to pick up on where new oil would be found, and decide on where it would go and what equipment would be needed – all in time for it to be delivered by the start of the dry season. Which actually meant, with a huge amount of guesswork, finalising designs ahead of getting the drilling results. Gratifyingly, with getting a stream of heads-up on assumptions before they went official, I was able to anticipate refinements in design each step of the way.

In this capacity I dealt with a number of suppliers, mainly from America. A pump salesman called me from the Federal Palace Hotel and asked me to come straight away. Strange as that was, it being more normal for them to come to my office, it got even odder when I reached the reception and, instead of finding him in the lobby, had to call his room. He asked me to come up. On knocking on his door, he opened it ajar to see it was me and then flung it open to pull me in. He was a big Texan but nervous as hell as he relayed things, 'They're all black!' His shock was all over his face, as he told how he'd come through customs and immigration, travelled in a taxi and then again when he'd arrived at the hotel.

The social life was good, our duplex apartment in a small un-gated compound – few compounds were gated – was comfortable. The only complaint: noisy bedroom air conditioners, to which nobody could acclimatise.

The local Times published the daftest of stories – such as a thief who was chased by traders in a market. When they caught up with him, he'd changed into a goat. Disquietingly for us, they published when public executions were to take place – death by firing squad – on the beach just in view from our windows. We never swam there!

We'd bought our first new car, on our last trip to London, and when it arrived the VW Beetle was a joy to drive. We were caught in a flash flood out at the Apapa Docks one day, and to our amazement were able to keep driving when all other cars had come to a stop in the deep flowing water. The Beetle floated and its wheels drove us forward like a paddle steamer. Pam had to be mobile and, there being no public transport for us to use, she naturally had the Beetle in the week. To the amusement of our friends, I drove to work on a Honda mini bike – which was the size young kids fooled around on. My knees were up by my chin. It got me through the heavy traffic better than any of them, though. Pity about the rain. Barry Shimmield, a friend and colleague, bought it off us when we left and I believe he brought it to the UK.

There were several clubs that were fun and we joined the Lagos Yacht Club. We'd enquired about buying a boat with another engineer, Jan Grevink, and how we should learn to sail. The previous owner's answer was brisk, 'Just get in. Find out as you go.'

Funnily enough, I later asked a Nigerian engineer to come out for a sail and he laughed in answer, 'What? No! My family would have to sacrifice a goat to pray for my safe return.' I'd experienced an island village in the swamps near Port Harcourt, when parents with children were preparing to cross a wide creek in canoes. A couple of children misjudged their footings and fell in the water. Men struggled to reach them by wading in while holding onto a canoe. They made quite a deal of rescuing the kids and I realised then that despite living a riverine existence none of them could swim. I saw how villagers in the swamps, on other islands, waded or doggy paddled at best. Muscle density could have been a factor, making them less buoyant, and those waters were in no way as salty as the sea. I've read since that that's not uncommon around the world. It's not even that uncommon among seasoned European fishermen who spend their whole lives working at sea.

Grevink and I bought a shearwater catamaran that he and I raced, but not before facing the perils of the club. A "making tide", when the flow is upstream, pushed water fast under the low bridge that connected Ikyoi Island, just where the club's boat ramps were, and Victoria Island. In a light breeze any boat lacking headway, whether launching from the ramps or returning to them, would end up hard against the arch and hoping for the rescue boat to get there really fast. Boats that the current pushed underneath risked a broken mast.

Wednesdays and Saturdays were race days. Sundays were family days when Pam, Natasha and I would sail up Badagry Creek to any number of beaches on the seaward side of that shore. Or we'd sail out of the harbour, in a strong breeze racing powerboats doing thirty knots, to where the club had a house on a popular beach just outside of the breakwater.

A major event, a two to three day one, was the Badagry Race; which the club has held annually since 1932 (to the present day), the only break being during the Biafran war. Over 140 km long it boasts being one of the longest dinghy sailboat races

111

(inland) in the world. Scores of boats sailed night and day, along the creek that runs intra-coastal to Badagry, and back. The winners in each class were judged on 'sailing' time; the time not spent asleep at anchor in unfavourable tides and winds.

I crewed on a dinghy in my first race and as darkness fell, overwhelmingly quickly on that moonless night in the tropics, we switched on torches to see our way. The breeze had not yet dropped as we spied a fish trap, its v-shaped structure just protruding above the surface dead ahead. The skipper whispered, 'Hold your torch on the sail.' We sailed on, straight at the mouth of the trap. 'Ready about,' he whispered 'torches off, going about.'

Moments later we heard, 'Bastards!' and much else, from the boat that had hoped for a free tour through the maze of traps with my more experienced skipper. His salutary ruse had worked; there was just enough wind to carry on racing, but with the tide now on the make the other two were snared.

I skippered our shearwater catamaran the next year, with Pam my crew and a beautiful sky overhead. Quickly on a broad reach, we braced our feet under straps and arched backwards into the stiff breeze. Sails now taught, the hull under us bucked clear out of the water. Our charge was up and alive with the hull below us seemingly skimming the surface, like a dragon dipping its wing there, while the wind howled over sails and strummed at the rigging with an adrenalin infusing hum. From the elevated viewpoint I could see we were well placed at the front of so many sheets bristling in the sun. We were right up with the leaders of the race and in with a chance against the lightweight tornado catamarans that always beat us in gentler winds. A place in the famed Badagry Race was in sight.

It took no time for us to cross the wide harbour and enter the creek, where the tacks were short from bank to bank. We were still up with the leaders and heading at a tree-lined shore, waiting to the last before tacking, when Pam screeched out, 'Look!' and pointed to the stern just near us. The windward rudder was dangling limp there, useless. Its mounting had broken with the force put on it. But I couldn't move, couldn't let the wind out of the mainsail. Hooked on the race I couldn't contemplate dropping out, as we careered toward the trees. Pam screeched again, 'Stop! Please stop!' One hand feeling every movement of the tiller and one tuned to the tension in the mainsail this was our race, our moment. In time-lapse slow motion I took in the wall of trees and the vision of going about rudderless in the water. And that was it, she was right. It was over. The race was over, for us. I turned us into the wind, away from the shore, and felt as deflated as the hull flopping onto the surface and the mainsail flapping idly. There was no hurry as we ran before the wind in silence, with no need for a spinnaker to speed us to the clubhouse. Pam was my soulmate and for me Carlo Collodi's Jiminy Cricket in the face of danger. We were good; we laughed.

Naively, at the outset of another wet season, I set about painting the hull in a garage using aerosol cans. I was due to visit colleagues in Port Harcourt but, when the light aircraft landed, I collapsed to the ground from the plane's steps. The next I knew, a large black nurse had taken my naked body into a shower at the clinic to get my temperature down. She did that frequently. Dr Peterson informed me that I had an unusual non-endemic form of pneumonia and, as such, it was not responding to antibiotics. He'd tried all the usual ones and none worked. He equated the area of my lungs to a tennis court and said I'd lost the equivalent of the serving area. He read and read, sleeplessly for five days while with a temperature of over 100° F the nurse showered me constantly. Pam couldn't get Shell-BP to fly her and Natasha there – only company flights were available – which might have been because I was critical. Finally, Peterson found an antibiotic that did work. A month later an article in Time magazine revealed what he had deduced, that the pneumonia had been an *extremophile* in the paint I'd used and the aerosol had weakened resistance in my lungs.

I owed my life to Peterson's diligence and returned to the social life in Lagos with gusto. Good food and drink was still hard to come by but lunchtimes I occasionally spent at a Lebanese restaurant with friends David Wells and Manfred

Whitman. They'd first introduced themselves to Pam, with a bottle of Champagne in a bucket that they'd swam up to her with in Umukoroshe. The restaurant owner had discovered that fishing boats discharging their catches at the Apapa Docks were discarding an odd creature with claws that got into their nets. We dined on lobster with Muscadet wine. Hmm, the joy!

Around that time we did an amazing thing with our Beetle. On being invited to a party in Port Harcourt, for friends to properly say goodbye to us, we drove there and back. We then took off on holiday, joining my sister Carolyn, husband David and daughters Kyle and Lisa in Milan. We'd all booked to go skiing in Verbier except, just before leaving Umukoroshe, Pam dislocated her knee when we were playing tennis. Then, on the very day we arrived in the Alps, David twisted his ankle. Since the girls were all very young, Natasha was just five, Carolyn insisted on taking them to the kids' slopes. That left just myself to ski higher up; but the exhilaration I felt was, well, fantastic and every bit what I got out of competitive sailing.

We flew from Milan to Malta, where we enjoyed the people so much that we bought a newly built apartment in Marsascala Bay. From there we flew to Tripoli to connect with an Aeroflot flight, which in the event was snowbound in Prague. We had to stop over in a hotel and, when passing through the airport, the Libyan customs confiscated a bottle of Napoleon Brandy from my case. Well OK, no bother, that was the law of the land. On leaving the next day I asked if I could get it back, as they'd previously told me would be the case, and, expecting nothing, they took me to a cupboard in an office. The doors opened to reveal shelves full of broken bottles of spirits and, right there, in the middle, my bottle of golden gleaming liquid was the only one still intact. They handed it back to me. Possibly my acquiescence had gone down better than the belligerent protests of others?

We had one more holiday while working in Lagos and spent that in Malta, joining my parents who were also vacationing there.

The Black Scorpion

By now the war had been over for well over three years but nevertheless the night curfew in Lagos persisted. Impossible! We couldn't have that! All the stressful times we'd been through still needed an out. We expats ignored it. A favourite spot for us was the Bacchus nightclub, Ikoyi, where we'd most often see the night through, occasionally until dawn. I see that it's still a leading nightspot of Lagos, which at that time was run by two Lebanese brothers who founded it. The DJ's music was always loud, the bar packed, the dance floor pulsating and crowded and there was hardly anywhere to sit.

One night Pam and I had enjoyed the company of friends including Barry Shimmield and wife Val, also another colleague Len Ogden and wife Val. On leaving we crossed Awolowo Road to our VW Beetle. I was waving back to Doreen, the Engineering Manager Red Beare's wife who'd been with us when, suddenly, a black Mercedes stopped between us. A short, slight man with big ears and dressed in civilian clothes left the car and strode over to where I stood with my arm on the car door. Reaching me he shouted incoherently, furiously. Then he started to chop at my arm with the side of his hand. I reasoned with him, or tried to, but failed hopelessly. His bashing continued unabated. Finally, irritated, I did something I'd only ever done one other time. Attacked by four young men out to impress girlfriends – in a back street of London, when two friends of mine disappeared and a policeman down the road also vanished – I defended myself with a clip that broke a nose and dispelled them all. Now, once again, I retaliated, to stop the shouting. I slammed my fist hard into this man's face.

Instantly, two soldiers grabbed hold of me and marched me to a van on the road. I tripped on the curb and the sergeant held me fast, while whispering, 'No, no dei resist.' He was pleading with me to go quietly as they ushered me into the vehicle. As we drove off I saw and heard Pam through the rear window. She had the civilian by the collar and was screaming, 'What are you doing with my husband? Where are you taking him?'

The van stopped outside a bungalow, the sergeant motioning me to get out, again his voice pleading, 'No resist. You dei go dis way.' The two soldiers ushered me through the front door, as the civilian arrived. They led me to an armchair to which the small man indicated. That done, they left.

'I will have you flogged!' The civilian bellowed, the best he could with his small voice. He then called for his maid and ordered her to bring him wine. Waiting, he said nothing, and just scowled. When the wine was poured he again addressed me sternly but with a curious civility, 'This is South African.' He perhaps expected some recognition on that point. 'It's banned here, you know,' he added.

My senses weren't getting the implication of this comment but then, I thought, of course apartheid. Nigeria had imposed sanctions on South Africa. Still, as a captive, whose wife was fretting out there somewhere, chat wasn't uppermost on my mind. I chose to be mute, rather than enflame things by babbling nonsensically.

'I will have you stripped and flogged!' he bellowed again before sipping the red wine. Thoughts of him doing as he said were doubtless in his head, not mine, as the moment dragged out. I refrained from thinking anything. Eventually, with his big ears comically flanking his head, he turned expressionless to me, 'Would you like to try some?'

'Yes,' I considered my response so as not to seem anxious or rather, as I reflect now, to sustain a measure of silent composure, 'Please.'

He called for his maid to bring another glass. When that was poured, he asked, 'It's good?'

'Yes, thank you,' I wasn't in the mood for savouring wine but, as I recall, it was a good full-bodied vintage.

He stood up, went to the bathroom and returned to really shout at me, 'Look!' he was fuming as he shook his fist and pointed to his cheek, now swelling, 'Look! I will have you taken to Dodan Barracks and flogged!' He sat down again, still fuming. I couldn't know, couldn't possibly comprehend, anything about the man or this incident. Except, the army had come out of nowhere back there on Awolowo Road. This had to be a high-ranking officer.

'I know. When does your work permit expire?'

'Next week, as it happens,' though doubly perplexed I could have added that I was in the process of getting it extended. But again I thought better of speaking up.

'I'll have it renewed!' came his extraordinary response. I don't recall why anymore but somehow I now judged this officer to be more than high-ranking. 'You know, I read Ojukwu's book.'

'What? Where did that come from?' was all I could think.

He went on to speak about having defeated him, in the context of battling as heads of armies against each other. I was sensing déjà vu, with the NEPA manager in Warri. Once again I was in the dark on what had gone on and could contribute absolutely

119

nothing. I do remember being surprised by what he said next regarding Ojukwu, 'He was right. I'd not agree with everything. But he was right about the injustices and inequalities of political elites.'

At that moment, and on reflection it's good that it wasn't any time later – I wasn't the man he could offload on, I had nothing to offer – a pretty Australian girl came in, 'Hey Benjy, you have a nice place here.' I gathered later that she was a casual girlfriend of his.

She was followed by a Nigerian civilian; who turned out to be his solicitor and who'd been in the Mercedes with him. He tried to defuse the situation, cordially, without saying much. Next, one of the Bacchus owners strode in with more to offer, 'Hey Benjy, you could open a nightclub here. It's nice how you've decorated here.' This was becoming like a French farce.

Now with no hint of malice my captor waved his hand at me, 'Go.' He motioned to the bathroom. There I could see that my tie, blazer and hair were dishevelled. I didn't register then, but others have made the connection since, about the expat wife he'd left screaming on the road. My wife. He'd maybe been worried about her making trouble. At the outset his solicitor might have cautioned him about who we were, a senior employee of Shell-BP and his wife. And the Engineering Manager's wife had seen everything. Could they have turned this nutter off his Dodan Barracks flogging spree that he'd been ranting about?

On my return to the living room he ordered his soldiers to take me back to my car. My grotesquely gracious host then had a parting word for me, 'You must come back tomorrow, for dinner.'

I nodded, for want of anything as courteously as to an officer of the law, and left with my guards. The ordeal behind me, my full attention was on making sure Pam was okay. My car wasn't at the club, naturally, so I had the soldiers take me to my home. The car was there but my wife wasn't. That was it, time to release these men and I suspected their relief in that. With nothing to go on, I went straight to the apartment of Shell-BP's Personnel Manager, not far from our home on Victoria Island. Mrs Page opened the door, as shocked as if a ghost stood before her.

I introduced myself before saying, 'I'm sorry to bother you at this hour. But do you know where my wife is?'

'Oh,' there was a tremor in her voice, as she ushered me in, 'would you like a cup of tea?'

'Thank you, no,' I was respectful but on a mission, ' Do you know where Pam is?'

'Are you sure you won't have a cup of tea?'

'No, really, where is Pam?' I beseeched, as calmly as I could.

To put some context here, this was not a good time for communications. She couldn't make a call, landlines didn't work and mobiles hadn't been invented yet. In hindsight, fully dressed at this late hour, she'd obliviously been fretting about the incident for which her husband had been called away. The last thing she'd expected was for the victim of the night to appear at her door. 'They've gone to the British Cultural Attaché.'

Pam had martialled people right at the top, to rescue her man. Mrs Page told me where to find the Attaché's office, downtown in Lagos. I heard later that at his house, where they'd first gone, he'd opened the door still in his underpants. His wife was there too.

I parked and took the lift, which arrived at a floor exclusive to the Attaché. The lift door opened to reveal Mr Page with Pam, and the Attaché in full ceremonial dress – gold braid, medals, possibly even a sword strapped on. By his whole demeanour, I saw he was ready to storm Dodan Barracks and demand my release. Except they all had the same expression that Mrs Page had: I was a ghost.

When Pam and I finally reached our car, that's when I suddenly went to jelly. All the time I'd hung in there, focused on getting through, and now that the incident was over the adrenalin that had sustained me drained away faster than air from a deflating balloon.

The next day I attended a debriefing with Shell-BP directors – one of whom was Engineering Director Eddie Farnkle, to whom my boss Brian Cook once asked me to present plans for buying a million pounds worth of pumps.

I learnt that my abductor was none other than Brigadier Benjamin Adekunle, the legendary Black

Scorpion. I was told he'd been given 30 days solitary at Sandhurst for appearing on parade with a haircut he'd bizarrely cultivated. The view was that this had enflamed his attitude towards Brits. Certainly the man was complex, with a history of mistreating Anglo-Saxons, or whites. The directors related how Adekunle had stopped an Australian diplomat and his wife on the road. He made the husband step down into a storm ditch and made his wife face the other way while he fired his revolver. It turned out that he hadn't shot the man but had him taken to Dodan Barracks where he had him flogged in front of her.

'What should I do about the invitation to dinner?' I asked.

I was informed that the man was known to be on drugs. His actions by my car were certainly indicative of that. I've since learnt his corps was suspected of running a hemp ring. 'He mightn't even remember offering an invitation,' I was advised. It was up to me, and my wife.

I have no idea now, why, but Pam and I went to his house the next evening. Mad! Sure enough he hadn't remembered. We began a conversation with no prospect of a meal and no idea of what to discuss. Then the lights went out. Daft, this was daft! Anyway I went with him to his fuse box, switched the lights back on, and then Pam and I excused ourselves and left.

A little while later Pam and I joined friends on a paddle steamer jazz boat in the harbour. On arrival, a voice called out, 'George! Join us.' It was Adekunle, with friends. I have to admit, I would have given him the benefit of the doubt. I might, subconsciously, have been intrigued to learn more about the man and at least gone over to exchange brief courtesies. Pam, defiant, wasn't having any of that. Grabbing my arm she pulled me away and that was the last we ever saw of the Brigadier.

He was forcibly retired shortly after.

A year later his boss, Head of State General Yakubu Gowon, was deposed by a coup and had to flee to Britain. His successor Brigadier Murtala Ramat Mohammed even initiated the transfer of the whole federal capital from Lagos to Abuja.

Adekunle died last year (2014).

Around the same time as Adekunle's retirement I was told Shell Expro, Shell's North Sea operation, wanted me assigned there. Life was tricky in Lagos; reports at social functions of robbery and injury among expats were increasingly common. One of Shell-BP's bachelor staff was missing at work for a couple of days, and was found dead in his apartment from cerebral malaria.

In another incident a colleague of mine was with his wife in their high-rise apartment, when a line squall blew the windows right through; luckily they'd crouched to the floor. Nevertheless, none of us were living in gated compounds with bars on doors and stairways as in China. And our six-year-old, Natasha, even played freely in our servants' quarters; we felt that safe she could be out of our sight.

One time, as we walked along a crowded pavement, and I chose to go between double-parked cars, a young black came up to me and tried to squeeze past. It was so ridiculous, the gap was clearly too small, that I grabbed his arm to tell him. To my astonishment my wallet was in his hand as I brought it up. He glanced to accomplices on the pavement, who ran away. All I could do was chastise him and let him go with no further fuss. He didn't fight back. Getting the police involved would have been a nightmare.

That was trivial in comparison to other crimes we'd been privy to. Yet, for all that we'd been through, that was the only civil crime in which we might have been the victims. On balance I was enjoying the work and, as a family, we were enjoying the sailing and such. But, it wasn't an option. We were relocating. Biafra and Nigeria were to be behind us now.

In a last act, we asked our steward about his ambition and heard how he'd hoped to become a photographer. I gave him my full set of Agfa equipment – a camera, tripod, lenses and some dark room equipment. We wished him success, meaning it sincerely.

~*~

15 A complex man, in a complex situation

May 1968 interview Stern Magazine, Germany:

Colonel Benjamin Adekunle a.k.a. the "Black Scorpion", Commander, 3rd Marine Commando Division, Nigerian Army –

On marching into the Port Harcourt area: *'We aim at everything that moves.'*

On entering the Ibo heartland: *'There we will aim at everything even if it is not moving'*

On European Humanitarian Assistance: *'In the section of the front that I rule—and that is the whole south front from Lagos to the border of Kamerun—I do not want to see the Red Cross, Caritas Aid, World Church delegation, Pope, Missionary, or UN delegation.'*

'I want to avoid feeding a single Ibo as long as all these people have not given up yet.'

On sympathy for the Ibos: *'I have learned a word from the British, which is "sorry"! That's how I want to respond to your question. I did not want this war but I want to win this war. Therefore I have to kill the Ibos. Sorry! The End.'*

I would like to reflect briefly on my encounter with the Black Scorpion. If I had known just a little of what I have gleaned since, I could have tried to make sense of that night – he has been likened to Macbeth in having murdered sleep, around that time.

Adekunle had openly abhorred the political class, the military elite, in Nigeria's bloody post-colonial struggles. The driving force behind his campaign successes was his mission to unify the fatherland, Nigeria – conscious that the succession of commanders in the Nigerian Army 3rd Division was exclusively Yoruba he (a Yoruba himself) had complained 'there are too many Yoruba under my command'. Yet, his convictions and there were many, made him dangerous then to those elite.

After the war he was promoted to Brigadier, reporting to the Commander-in-Chief of the Armed Forces, Head of State General Yakubu Gowon, and charged with ridding the Apapa Docks of its chronic congestion. The big demand for cement had prompted so many shipments that the vessels were queued out at sea for too long. Cargoes went off and some vessels had to be scuttled.

There was such huge disarray at the docks that Shell-BP, far from getting help by being in league with the Nigerian government, had to airlift cement to their drilling rigs.

However, I've learnt from Adekunle's published letters that, at the time of our encounter, he was under threat of being forcibly retired. If there was any truth in the myths about his defeating the enemy with the 'shock and awe' of slaughtering whole villages, none of that was uppermost in his thoughts right now. Instead, this Scorpion had sleepless forebodings over Gowon's plans for him. In his letters he even feared for his life.

So that, as the misadventure with me unfolded, and I suspect his solicitor had cautioned him of it at the outset, drugs or not he'd have feared provoking Gowon over mistreating a senior employee of Shell-BP and his wife. And this attractive wife, left on the road, had the fire of Boadicea.

I also suspect that his climb down over my hitting him – no one had ever done that before, apparently – in some small part had to do with the respect he held for the British West Africa administration. He was a product of that order – a complex man, in a complex situation, at a complex time. And Shell-BP's perception of him would have emanated from Gowon's offices. It might actually have been that, in that dire time for him, with my not buckling or flinching, some fond reminiscence of the Royal Military Academy Sandhurst (UK) was triggered

He had written about the respect he had for Sandhurst where he had trained, also the British forces in West Africa and the legacy Britain had left in India, where he had once served. By comparison he was appalled by the inhumanity he saw when serving with UN forces in the Congo.

The only hate in his writings was directed at the racism he had been subjected to on the streets of

Britain, which he abhorred between tribes in his own country but had not expected to find as a black man there. The British were transforming – as champions of modern sports, the arts and welfare – to the caring society we see today and where Nigerians have a far better standing today. The opening ceremony of the 2012 Olympic Games in London captured the essence of that transformation beautifully.

I would like to venture reflecting something more about Adekunle. Against the aspirations of ordinary people, in the moment of weakened social order that followed independence, the political elite that Adekunle and Ojukwu both abhorred took over. Bloodshed took over almost without exception, like a plague sweeping unfettered to spread greed and corruption round the world.

Ojukwu fought against it, losing everything his wealthy father had left to him. Adekunle fought with the elite, but might that be because he hoped to make change from within, in support of Nigerian unification – which he doubtless wanted for his Igbo wife too. Yet, in the process, somehow, he lost his direction? Is that what he had eluded to in talking to me?

None of what happened to Nigeria then and since, at the hand of elites, is pardonable. I'd had some grizzly insight to atrocities both sides had carried out. Yet, it seems to me that by far the darkest force in the Biafran War had to do with Cold War tactics. The greatest massacres occurred in the bombing raids on towns, schools, aid supplies and hospitals, of Soviet and Czechoslovak supplied planes flown (dispassionately?) by Egyptian mercenary pilots. A shame on humanity is that the Cold War legacy lives on and, wherever it does, it wrecks the hopes and aspirations of ordinary people.

The Soviets among others unaligned with UN peacekeeping objectives have complicated another outside influence: that of extremist aspirations in the Islamic world. Some years later as the foreign partner in Form Arabia Furnishing Co, Kuwait, I was in the office of Sheik Moubarak, a member of the most important family after the ruling Sabahs, to negotiate renewing the rent for our showroom premises. The man was well dressed in a white dishdash and very eloquent in English. He asked me to wait while he completed discussions with a group of Kuwaitiis; which was revealing in that he referred to those bedouins as low-lifes.

Most significantly, a TV was playing to one side and as we spoke the news caught both of us, now alone together, by complete surprise. The Berlin wall was coming down. After gathering our stunned thoughts I simply observed, 'Wow! That's one superpower gone.' We exchanged startled looks. 'Which leaves just one?' Which, that power being America, I presumed to be a relief.

He astonished me with words I will never forget, '*It's our turn now!*' That was all he said. It was impulsive, I am sure, and possibly a personal reflection only, and yet once again I found myself

130

unable to respond. Unable to engage in a dialogue that, this time, could have become unproductive in the context of the business agenda I had to complete.

Shortly after, in quick succession, there came: The Gulf War, Bosnian War and the USA led UN action in Somalia. Slightly later Islamic terrorism began in the Philippines, slaughter over Sharia Law started in Nigeria and then there was 9/11 in New York. It's been chaos among factions unaligned with the UN. Boko Haram had its beginnings back then and has gone on to massacre countless thousands unchecked.

How is any of this relevant? The fight against archaic, fundamental Islamists in the North of Nigeria is well known, as are China's colonial style policies. However, I believe there are still lessons to be learned from the Biafran War, when the Soviet military ruthlessly aided and abetted the genocidal massacres of Nigeria's post independence political elites. That support was irrefutably medieval and, unlike Europe's tsunami transformation to a caring society post World War II, the Soviets show little sign of moving forward yet.

~*~

16   Tyres smoking on the roadside

A decade after leaving Nigeria I frequently visited West Africa to offer the services of a Texan employer, Creole Productions Services International, to oil companies. On my first trip back to Lagos, arriving in the early hours, I walked out into the dark with very few passengers; to find the airport surrounded by army vehicles and heavily armed soldiers scrutinising me. I reached a taxi, glad to be moving away from the scene and along the expressway I knew would take me to my hotel.

Relief turned to alarm when the driver went down a slip road and along unlit back streets. For long minutes I refrained from belying any inner feelings, rather relying on trust, an ordeal that ended with him stopping in a small, unlit forecourt. He got out and moved to a wall. He'd gone to a petrol pump, an old model that he pumped by hand.

Prior to travelling I had visited a doctor, hoping for a procedure to rid me of hemorrhoids that were paining me. He told me to 'live with it' and in time the problem might go away. Okay, he wasn't to know I'd soon be in a jeep with a hard suspension, a driver with a knack of finding potholes, and every bounce would have my eyes watering with pain.

What got my attention was a stack of tyres smoking on the roadside. On enquiring about it, the answer was that it was how villagers dealt with thieves. Tyres were pulled over the head, encasing the culprit, and then set alight. Better that than the likelihood of involving corrupt policemen.

Back at the hotel I went to the accounts office, the only place with international lines. Other guests were trying to get a line out and I eventually had hold of a phone. 'No line. No line,' I was fretting wanting to talk with Natasha and inevitably lost my temper, 'Don't you have any line that works?'

'No! You dei wait. Try again!' The man was unsympathetic.

I tried, and tried; infuriated by their attitude I let fly, 'Why you be so angry?'

A silence fell on the room, aggression hanging on the air. Except one of the girls used a more demure, understanding tone, 'It not be our way.' Her sudden softness stilled everyone. 'We come to the city and that be how it is here.' That struck a chord, with me knowing the desperate conditions millions were suffering.

Pyles were a bane right up to my arriving back at the airport, where I discovered that seats were not allocated. Desperate to get an exit seat with leg-room I moved to the departure gate ahead of everyone. On being told we could board I dashed onto the tarmac and eyed the plane with steps to it just ahead of us. As fast as I could, walking with clenched cheeks like Hercule Poirot, I led a long line of passengers. Except that wasn't the right plane. I looked about to see another, and waddled that way again followed by the line of passengers.

We stood where we expected there to be steps and instead the captain slid back his cockpit window to call out over us, 'Bring some steps here, so we can leave!'

Another visit was to Kinshasa, the Congo, where music interspersed with political messages played out from roadside loudspeakers. Streets were in deplorable disrepair and in the place of traffic and bustling activity there were military vehicles shrouded in darkness.

Conversing with anyone would have required a better command of French than I had. In a taxi, I did hear Muhammad Ali (formerly Casius Clay) on the radio. He'd just been asked, in English, about winning the fight with George Foreman there, the famed "Rumble in the Jungle". The presenter now asked, 'So, how do you feel about being here in Africa?'

'Well,' his retort was as swift as ever, 'I'm just glad my great granddaddy didn't miss the boat!'

Back at the hotel I got news that my flight had been cancelled. I would have to travel the next day. Most devastatingly I couldn't get a line out, to let my daughter in boarding school know I wouldn't be arriving as planned for the weekend. We'd enjoyed good moments on my visits; with front row seats at the pantomime Pirates of Penzance in which the star, Spike Milligan, called out for reinforcements to fight the brigands. Those visions were there with me in the taxi to the airport the next day. He had held his hand out to Natasha and pulled her onto the stage to fight alongside him. The taxi moved slowly through roadblocks and we were almost stationary as we passed men being lined up. For public execution?

It was chaos at the airport, an anxious throng of Congolese packing the check-in hall offered no prospect of my getting to the desk. Delays on the road had robbed me of time and the flight was about to leave. I managed to get the attention of the local SAS (Scandinavian Airlines) staff who beckoned me to pass my stuff to them. To my astonishment black hands held out to me and I gave my suitcase and passport to the crowd. Hoping my trust was not misplaced I watched my valuables being passed over heads. My passport, ticket and boarding pass all came back to me the same way and I rushed through the departure gate just in time.

When I finally arrived at the public school (in the UK those are private schools) I was told that Natasha had waited all the previous day at the gate, insisting to teachers that I was coming. That faith, shattered by events, broke my heart. I don't think I ever managed to make up to her for that.

~*~

The Author

Born in World War II Asmara, Eritrea, I was not a healthy arrival. My godfather, Brigadier Stephen Longrigg, British Administrator of the region, arranged for me to be seen by an Italian doctor, a WWII prisoner of war (POW). Paid for his services with a packet of cigarettes, the man diagnosed my inability to digest breast milk as a constriction of the stomach. It was so small even condensed milk, the only alternative, couldn't sustain me.

The prognosis was hopeless. But, they'd not reckoned on my mother's persistence. From colonial stock, her father was a tea planter in Ceylon, she fed me non-stop until I won through. (Boy, do I still like condensed milk!).

My schooling was at Les Petit Oiseau (Rome), Roaring Brook Elementary School (NY), Wellington School (Somerset UK), and Northampton College of Advanced Technology (City University, London).

I won a scholarship with Crompton Parkinson (Hawker Siddeley) and, on graduating with a BSc.MechE(Hons), I joined Shell International as a Chartered Engineer MIMechE.

Today, I am a writer and publisher.

Other 2013-14 GBP Publications

'Contrary to popular stereotypes Captain George P. Boughton relates how, apart from the elements or rather because of the elements, seamen on sailing vessels were highly respectful of each other as well as of their colour and religious persuasions.'

'Seafaring – The Full Story' by Captain George P. Boughton

The Captain saw nothing of the millennia-long slave trade. His time at sea in the 19th century began some three quarters of a century after slave trafficking on the high seas was policed by the West Africa Squadron of the British Royal Navy.

As much a one-man reminiscence as it is an elegy for a forgotten way of life, it's not hard to imagine a gravelly voiced Boughton recalling the era of the "large sailing ships" and why the world stopped being a better place when they were forced off the sea.

Juliette Foster, Surrey Life magazine 2015

"His book is genuine sea salt...warm colours of Mr Shoesmith's pictures accord well with the romantic story" of days before steamships

Times Literary Supplement

Seafaring

The Full Story

isbn 9780957672826

"one of the best books on life at sea that have been published for many a day"

Lloyds List & Shipping Gazette

"recalls emotions [on sea-life] *that have fleeted from the minds of most"*

The Spectator

"This book is stamped with the personality of a thorough seaman, the sea-breezes [and chanties] stir in its pages"

Blue Peter Journal, AT Stewart Commander
Royal Navy

Oil is popularly perceived of as a dirty fuel. There's no doubt that it pollutes the air and potentially it can do that to waterways too. That needs to change.

But at it's dirtiest, spread out over the oceans, it can kill more than individual life forms. It can stop all life – it's most likely done that in the past – by shutting down the carbon and water cycles that vitally re-terraform the land.

The solution: get it out of the ground. NOW. By all means, which includes fracking. The facts are revealed in the novel *DeepStorm OutTack* by George S Boughton.

DeepStorm

OutTack

isbn 9780957297081

From Earth's overcrowded megacities a new generation must rise...or die

By the 2060s – the march of megacities across the globe has finally stopped but the population must still grow.

Now mankind turns its eyes to space – building the Near Earth Territories and peopling them with youngsters DNA-primed to survive there.

When a planet destroying cosmic disturbance bears down on the Earth, a team of Territories' researchers scrambles to respond with enhanced talents and hard science.

More than just science fiction *DeepStorm OutTack* is based on a decade of intensive research.

Enjoy the story but heed the warning – mankind could go the way of the dinosaurs.

Lightning Source UK Ltd.
Milton Keynes UK
UKOW04f0323220917
309664UK00001B/39/P